Breaking Into My Life

michelle dickinson-moravek

BREAKING INTO MY LIFE

growing up with a bipolar parent and
my battle to reclaim myself

Rudy ♡
Thank you for you
amazing support ♡
Love, Michelle

Printed in the United States of America

First Printing, 2018

ISBN 978-0-9888262-7-4

Contact information:
Michelle Dickinson-Moravek
P.O. Box 413, Kenilworth, NJ 07033
breakingintomylife@gmail.com

Publisher: Incubation Press
Designer: Lieve Maas, Incubation Press

To Eddie, my rock.

TABLE OF CONTENTS

ACKNOWLEDGEMENTS

I would like to express my deepest gratitude to the many people who saw me through the writing of this book.

First and foremost, I would like to thank my husband, Eddie, for standing beside me always and especially during the many hours of writing this book. He provided me with love and support, discussed ideas, reminded me of events I tried to forget, and prevented several wrong turns.

Secondly, I would like to thank my writing coach, Linden Gross, who helped guide me and helped extract the rich experiences, wrapped in raw emotions, that represented mental illness from the lens of a child. Linden, your partnership has been a blessing. I am so grateful for your wisdom and support.

Thank you also to Lieve and Scott at Incubation Press for your amazing talents. And thank you David Rosell for so generously sharing your experience and wisdom.

I would like to thank my dear godmother Aunt Muriel for her love and support throughout this entire process. I would also like to express my profound appreciation to my loving and supportive step-mom, Carole Dickinson, who has always been there for me.

I also want to thank my family including Jae, Trish and all of our family and friends who supported and encouraged me in spite of the long and emotional journey. I would like to thank those who eagerly helped me in the early stages of this book including Mike, Janet, Lina, and Koshy. And, thank you Brayson for allowing me to capture your powerful interaction with Tony Robbins during our program together.

Thank you to my many high school friends and their families for allowing me to share some of my most fond memories with you.

Finally, with profound gratitude I want to thank my extraordinary work family at Johnson & Johnson for their wisdom, guidance, and unwavering support. Thank you Ruby, Craig, Geralyn, Linda, Sarah, Hussani, Marlene, Christine and so many others who generously encouraged me along the way. I am proud and very honored to get to work alongside you as we strive to elevate the conversation around mental illness.

I beg forgiveness of all those who have been with me over the course of the years and whose names I have failed to mention. You're in my thoughts and my heart.

PART 1
Growing Up With Mom

CHAPTER 1

Doorknob

MY HANDS ARE SWEATY, AND MY STOMACH is twisting like a French braid that's pulled too tight. It's 3:25 p.m. and I'm just getting home from school. My heart sinks as I reach for the doorknob. I know I'm in trouble. I'm ten minutes late.

Why did I walk so slowly? I ask myself.

At the age of thirteen, I know the rules all too well. If I don't get home from school by 3:15 p.m., Mom locks me out of the house. There's a good chance I'll be spending the next hour or more sitting on the driveway's cold pavement as punishment for being late. I take a deep breath and turn the knob.

Crap! It's locked.

What's my excuse? I ask myself with a sense of panic. *I need an excuse.*

I ring the bell. Mom comes to the door. She pushes back the window drape and looks at me through the glass. Her makeup and silky chestnut hair are done perfectly today, and she's wearing her favorite paisley shirt. Today is her bowling day.

She draws back her freshly painted-red lips into an angry scowl. She opens the door and points her pink manicured finger in my face.

"You're late," she says in her all-too-familiar accusatory tone, punctuating each word.

I follow her inside the Lysol-smelling house. She walks through the kitchen and into the dining room, giving me her back the entire way. Everything is perfectly situated in its proper place. The wood dining room table shines from being polished and a freshly starched crisp doily runs down its center beneath a silk floral arrangement. The afternoon sun spills through the lace-curtain-dressed windows and the louvers of the wooden shutters onto the freshly vacuumed dark-green carpet.

"Mom, I'm sorry. My teacher asked me to stay after school to help her, so I did."

"It doesn't matter, Michelle. You know that you're to be in this house by 3:15," she says firmly.

In that moment I realize that how I choose to respond will either set her off even more or actually temper her bad mood. How I react will dictate how my entire afternoon will go. How I react will potentially make her sick. I know that if I act up or do anything to irritate her, I'll contribute to her having a nervous breakdown. Again.

Michelle, you've got to say the right thing this time, I say to myself. *Think, think, think!*

Fortunately for me, I have learned how to manage her moods. When I spot her latest project out of the corner of my eye, I grab the lifeline.

"Mom, is that a new craft you're making? Can you show me what it is?"

Her face slightly relaxes and the anger seems to fade. Whew! I managed to play it right this time. Close call.

Yesterday I was late, but her reaction was completely different. When I got home at 3:45 p.m., the door was unlocked.

"Hi, honey," Mom said, greeting me with a smile.

Even so, I worried that she was going to scold me for being tardy. When it comes to Mom, smiles don't always mean what they normally do. But she didn't get angry. Instead, I could see that she was happy to see me.

"Why don't you run real quickly to George's Corner Store to get some chocolate marshmallow ice cream and Snickers candy bars?" she said.

I love chocolate and I knew she was going to share these treats with me. Having a moment like that with her is even better than chocolate. I wish I would get that reaction daily. Or even once a week. But I don't.

Every day after school that back door looms over me. I never know what to expect. *Is Mom going to be in a good mood or bad mood?* I wonder. This single thought consumes my entire walk home every single day. It's amazing how many times you can repeat that question to yourself.

If she's in a good mood, I will talk to her about my day at school, I think. *If she's in a bad mood, I will try my hardest not to do or say anything stupid that causes her to be even meaner to me than she usually is when she feels this way.*

The closer I get to the house, the more I want to throw up. Which mom will I be coming home to?

Please, Lord, just let her be in a good mood today.

It hasn't always been like this. When I was just five years old, I had a mom who was happy and loving all the time.

"You're the light of your mom's life," my relatives would tell me.

I knew they were right. I was the center of her universe then. Mom had explained to me when I was very young that I had been adopted, a fact I should be happy about.

"That means that you're special," she said. "Your father and I chose you out of all the babies in the nursery. There wasn't another baby that was wanted more than you."

Those words, along with the way she doted on me during the day and kissed my forehead when she tucked me into bed at night, left me feeling extremely loved. The strong sense of warmth and deep contentment at home only got better when Nana was over.

I remember awakening to the smell of bacon one sunny Saturday morning. Dad was making his famous blueberry pancakes that day. Yum! I bounced downstairs in my footie pajamas ready for breakfast. I just loved Saturday mornings and not only because of Dad's pancakes and bacon. I knew Nana would be arriving from Newark for the weekend.

After breakfast, I dressed quickly.

"Come on, Michelle," Mom hollered. "Hurry up, we are going to be late! The train is about to arrive."

Teddy, our black poodle, and I piled into the cushy back seat of our Mercury Marquis with its long two-toned gray upholstery bench and flip-up armrest in the middle. Within minutes, we arrived at the downtown Westfield train station.

"There she is, Mom," I yelled in delight. "There is Nana! I can see her."

At the sound of Nana's name, Teddy began bouncing between the front and back seats of the car, almost as excited as me. When she climbed into the car, he kissed her entire face, nibbling on her lips out of excitement. He always got the first snuggle, but that was okay. Mine was coming.

"Hi, Nana!" I said. "I've missed you. I'm so happy you're here!"

"Hi, sweetheart! I've missed you, too!"

After we got home, we sat around the large square kitchen table situated just beneath the kitchen window up against the dark-red brick kitchen wall, Nana at the end and me tucked onto her lap with my legs dangling on top of hers. As Mom poured coffee for Nana and Dad, Nana hugged and kissed me, her arms wrapping even more tightly around me. Nana gives me anything I ask for, but at that moment I couldn't imagine anything better than getting her and my mom's undivided attention.

Sunday winter mornings in those days were equally great for me. Mom and I would lie on the oversized soft and snuggly area rug on the living room floor just in front of the fireplace playing with my Sunshine Family doll set and their cardboard dollhouse. The doll set was just like us, with a mother, a father and one blond-haired baby that could have been me.

I think back to us hanging out one morning in our matching nightgowns just playing and laughing together until we had to get ready for an afternoon birthday party. Mom dressed me up in my favorite pretty little swirl dress. I just love swirl dresses. When you spin around, the skirt takes flight. The dress I wore that day had all the colors of the rainbow. Once I pulled it over my head, Mom placed two small bows in my hair and helped me put on my nicest gold necklace. I felt like her little princess.

Yes, I remember being spoiled as a very little girl, spoiled in the sense that I got a lot of love and focused attention from my mom. Fear of my mom's unstable moods was not a factor in those days. I don't remember her ever being mean. Life was just calm and predictable back then.

Something changed when our family changed.

CHAPTER 2

New Siblings

"HAVE A SEAT, SWEETIE. Mommy has something to tell you," Mom says in a soft and gentle tone as she smiles at me. "In just a few days you're going to be getting a big brother and a big sister."

"Really?"

"Do you remember your cousins Mary and Ralph from Pennsylvania?" Mom asks.

"Sorta," I respond.

"Sweetheart, their daddy suddenly passed away from a heart attack and their mom is too sick to care for them. They need a place to live, so they are going to come here to live with us now. Is that okay?"

"Yes, yes, yes!" I exclaim. "When can they come?"

"Soon. In just a couple of days."

The news fills me with excitement. I don't have even an ounce of hesitation. Perhaps I've secretly longed for siblings because I'm a bit lonely at home as an only child.

The days just crawl by until they arrive. In anticipation of my new sister and brother's coming to live with us, I help Mom prepare their rooms and make their beds. I make sure my room is tidy and that all my toys are put back in the TV room toy closet. I can't wait to share my favorite games, dolls and dollhouse with them. I even helped Mom clean the house a little.

Finally, today is the big day. Dad and I sit at our oval wooden dining room table, the brightly lit chandelier hanging above our heads. Yesterday we were just a family of three, plus Teddy, our dog. And today, I'm getting a new big brother and a new big sister. Today, we will become a family of five.

"These are your new brother and sister, Mary and Ralph," Mom says as she leads them to the table from the doorway. They enter hesitantly, their hands folded in front of them and their heads down. Even at my age I can tell that these timid, shy kids feel positively gloomy. They sit down at the dining room table.

"I'm four," I say. "How old are you?"

"I'm seven," says Ralph.

"I'm ten," says Mary.

"Do you like to play games?" I ask them.

They both shake their heads *yes*. I can hardly contain myself. Today is the very best day—ever! Even better than Christmas. I can't wait to show my new siblings our entire house. I want to show them my bedroom and all my favorite toys. I'm going to take them outside to the yard and show them our jungle gym. Then I want to take them to our basement to show them my secret places to hide for hide-and-seek. I have my own playmates at home with me now. We will be able to play anytime we want. This is going to be so fantastic!

Mom is doing a lot of the talking. Dad sits at the end of the table, quietly smoking a cigarette. He doesn't say much to make my new brother and sister feel welcomed. My new siblings aren't saying too much, either, but they are enjoying Mom's homemade cookies and that seems to make them smile a little.

Morning comes after our first sleep as a family. We are seated together at the kitchen table to have breakfast as the smell of brewing coffee fills the room and the radio plays Mom's favorite oldie station. Her burning cigarette hangs off the ashtray on the table. Everyone seems to be in a good mood. Even Mary and Ralph are smiling.

Mom pours us each a bowl of Cheerios.

"Where is the sugar?" Ralph asks.

"We don't add sugar to our cereal *in this house*," Mom replies firmly, a clear emphasis on the last three words. Her tone indicates that there will be no negotiating. I have never heard Mom talk like this before. I can tell that Ralph is not happy with Mom's response. I watch his disappointed face as he eats the sugarless Cheerios.

Life at home continues to feel different with each passing day. So does Mom. Her new tone of voice is not a passing phase, and is accompanied by many new rules. Over the course of the next eight years with my new siblings, the rules that show up in our house increasingly tighten. And a mother I don't even recognize clings to these rules as a daily mechanism to control us and measure us against.

A number of months after my new siblings move in with us, Mom puts the *Pac-Man Fever* record on the turntable on the stereo in the foyer. I can hear the first record drop. The giant speakers hanging on the walls in the living room start to play the first song. I know this song and the record she is playing. We all know what this means—Mom is in a good mood.

She cranks up the volume and starts dancing around the living room. I can feel the living room start to vibrate from the bass in the song.

"'Cause I've got Pac-Man fever. It's driving me crazy," she sings. "I got Pac-Man fever, I'm going out of my mind!"

As she continues, she gets louder and louder. Feeding off Mom's energy, Teddy begins barking as he throws his squeaky toy into the air and then pounces on it. Even he can feel Mom's jovial, lighthearted spirit.

My brother, Ralph, watches from the bottom step of the staircase, and my sister, Mary, and I from our seat on the couch. Just an hour before, Mom was screaming at us for not putting our sneakers away in the shoe bin. Now, all that tension seems to melt away. Mom is no longer mad at us. A sense of happiness infuses the room.

Mom's behavior so illuminates us that we even start singing along with her. She likes that, too. A comfort begins to emerge as we sing and giggle, thoroughly enjoying our happy, smiling mom.

Just when it seems like nothing in the world can bother her, something drastically shifts in Mom's demeanor. Suddenly distracted by a seemingly random thought, she storms over to the stereo and quickly turns down the music. She is no longer singing. She glances at us sternly. A clenched jaw and firm, tight lips have swallowed her smile.

Our happy mom is gone. In her place, I quickly realize, is a mom who is quite angry. I can tell this even though I only see her back as she searches for lace doilies that were her mother's in a small teacart in our dining room.

"I know someone stole those doilies," she says. "This is why I don't like people in my house! They are looking to take my things!"

I have no idea what she is talking about because I've never seen them before.

She proceeds to speculate that other items from her teacart have also gone missing. With a growing sense of paranoia, she anxiously riffles through each drawer.

I stare at her in complete confusion.

"Where are my mother's doilies?" she demands to know.

Just moments earlier we were all feeling so happy and light-hearted. It was like we finally had permission to just relax and smile because Mom was happy. Stupid us. We should have never let our guard down.

"Didn't I tell you that you better have that room of yours picked up by dinnertime, young lady?" she yells at me, momentarily distracted from the missing teacart items. "What are you doing down here when you have a filthy room upstairs? Now get upstairs and clean it up!"

I head up to my room, confused to no end by the angry mom who showed up out of nowhere. How can my happy and fun mom be gone so soon? Her drastic mood swings make me feel like a plastic bag being tossed around in the wind.

As the months pass following my siblings' arrival, many different variations of my once even-tempered and calm mom show up. I recognize each new version of my mom less and less.

On the skimpy plus side, the stress stemming from Mom's behavior seems to have a way of pulling us together. Almost instantly I start to feel like my new siblings and I have established a connection together. I truly feel like they are my brother and sister now and that we have become a tight-knit family, the result of being constantly together. There is comfort in knowing that whenever I do something, so do they. Whether we climb on the jungle gym in the backyard or play games on the living room floor, I just love having them around.

My siblings, however, just don't seem nearly as happy as I am about being here with us. They are quiet, and most of the time they even seem a little sad.

Before long, I'm reminded that my brother and sister have their own mother, Edith, who is permitted to come for visits once a month. Even though she is not able to take care of them, it's clear that she loves them just by how she looks at them.

When the doorbell rings on visitation day, Mom greets Edith at the front door and lets her in. She shows her to the living room and calls for my brother, Ralph, and sister, Mary, to come downstairs from their rooms. A strange woman accompanies her again. Mom later tells me that she is with the state of New Jersey and must be here to supervise the visits.

Mary and Ralph both seem somewhat happy to see their mom, but they give her stiff hugs. I sense a cold distance.

Mom is cordial at best and quickly disappears into the kitchen, where she will stay for the entire visit apart from bringing the ladies two cups of tea. Any possible compassion has been eclipsed by her feeling Edith is directly responsible for the death of her cousin, my new siblings' father. So she never shows any kind of compassion toward her during all the years she visits our home.

There we sit in the living room on that initial visit, Edith and the woman from the state on the new fluffy couches and the three kids in a circle on the newly carpeted floor. The fireplace is not lit for the visit. Mom and Dad only light it when we have company over that we like, and we are not having that kind of company today. The only thing offering any warmth is a small cranberry candle on the coffee table that scents the air.

Despite the tension that even a four-year-old can discern, I just love being included, because Mary and Ralph are now my sister and brother. We play a board game together while Teddy curls up on the only sunlit piece of carpet in the room, adjacent to Mom's easy chair. Expressionless, my brother just stares at the game on the floor. He completely avoids making eye contact with his mom. He doesn't want to talk, either. It takes a lot for Edith to get him to say anything to her. My sister is suddenly acting shy and also avoids eye contact with Edith. Instead, she looks down and quietly plays with her doll once the board game is over.

The reunion with their mother is obviously quite painful for both my new siblings. That doesn't change with future visits. It's like they just don't know how to be with their mother anymore, given what they have been through and that they are now a part of a brand-new family.

When the visits end, they're even quieter than usual. Often, they just run up to their bedrooms for the rest of the day until they're called to dinner. My mom's tense abruptness toward Edith does not help an already uncomfortable and trying situation. Neither does the fact that when Edith finally leaves, Mom routinely exhales a sigh of relief and mumbles to herself, "Damn that woman. Thank God she is the hell out of here!"

After that first visit, Mom remains visibly annoyed for the rest of the day. We know to avoid her at all costs because we do not want to experience her reaction if we upset her. Anyone crossing her path when she feels like this can expect a tongue-lashing and swift backhand. This, too, doesn't change.

Luckily for all of us, these stressful visits don't happen too frequently, which is good because I hate seeing my brother and sister seeming so confused and withdrawn. I like it best when they're happy and fun and we can just play together and laugh.

We laugh a lot. Mary uses humor to shield Ralph and me from my mom's negativity. She speaks to me with a silly accent, making me giggle uncontrollably until my stomach starts to ache. I especially love that her tasks include giving me my nightly bath. She makes me the biggest and best baths ever, filling the tub to the top with endless bubbles to make bubble mustaches and bubble beards. As we try to talk, the bubbles slowly slide down our faces, making us laugh even more.

As I get older, I begin to really look up to her because she is so pretty, mature and smart. She is also just a very sweet and kind person. She becomes my best friend, and I love that the most about having a big sister.

I talk to her about everything I can't talk to Mom about before we fall asleep in our beautiful matching canopy beds adorned with draping red floral ruffled skirts that mirror our matching bedspreads. Tonight, we're imagining our lives as grown-ups when we get older.

"How many kids would you have?" I whisper.

"Two, I think."

"I think I'll also have two," I agree.

"I know our kids will play together and have lots of fun."

"We'll be able to do whatever we want and have lots of fun as adults," I say. "There won't be so many rules to follow because grown-ups don't have to follow all the rules kids do."

We aren't whispering quietly enough. Mom, who is sitting with Dad in the room immediately next to our bedroom, overhears us talking. All of a sudden, in the pitch-black darkness, she whips open our bedroom door.

"I told you both that it was time for bed. Now go to sleep!" she yells. "If I have to come in here again, I will make you stop talking."

She slams the door so loudly that I swear she's broken the hinges. But we aren't done with our conversation, so we continue to whisper, very quietly now, even though we know the possible repercussions.

"Where would you live?" I ask Mary. "Would you live in a big house? Would we live close to each other? I hope so."

She's quiet now because she fears Mom will come back. The last time we got in trouble for staying up, we both got slapped really hard and it stung so much that it was difficult to fall asleep.

That's not uncommon these days. Mom is determined to make us bend to her will.

CHAPTER 3

The Magic of Christmas

LIVING WITH NEW MOM COMES WITH its fair share of challenges, something my siblings and I quickly figure out. Thankfully, Christmas is just around the corner.

"Christmastime is simply magical in our house," I tell Mary and Ralph.

I know they don't believe me, but they'll see. Mom loves the holidays so much, she literally takes days to create the perfect Christmas wonderland in almost every room of our house. For starters, she puts up five different trees. The one in the dining room is snow covered with white lights and clear plastic icicles. The kitchen tree is decorated with multicolored lights and miniature kitchen utensils. Our giant Christmas tree in the living room, which is topped with a bright-yellow star, extends as high as the ceiling. Buried in the tree, a bird ball sings the same sound over and over, as if a bird is perched inside.

Next to the tree, the garland-adorned fireplace has a mantel filled with tiny winter figurines. On the coffee table in the center of the room, perfectly spaced tiny snowmen surround a homemade yule log with tiny candles. As if that weren't festive enough, Mom decorates the staircase's wooden banister with lights, and weaves a shiny garland through every spindle of the staircase. When the tree, fireplace, coffee table and banister are all lit, a cozy little Christmas sanctuary comes to life.

That refuge, which extends past the decorations to the feel and function of our household, lasts for the whole holiday. It's like stepping into an alternate reality, especially because Mom and Dad spare no expense at Christmastime.

Just as I predict, Mary and Ralph can scarcely believe how the holidays shape up. And although I know what to expect, neither can I. By the time Christmas morning arrives, we're all bursting just waiting to see what Santa bought us. The smell of Dad's Christmas bread baking in the oven awakens me. I sneak a peek at the living room by draping myself over the upstairs railing. The fireplace is crackling and presents are piled on the floor in front of the Christmas tree. Wow!

In our matching Christmas pajamas, Mary, Ralph and I wait at the top of the stairs for Mom to come get us. That's the ritual. She lines us up at the top of the landing—first me, then Ralph, then Mary in order of size.

"Close your eyes," she says, placing our hands on one another's shoulders. Then, holding my hand, she slowly leads us down the steps. All I can hear is the camera clicking as Dad snaps away and Bing Crosby plays on the record player. With our eyes still shut, Mom positions each of us. The anticipation of what is coming fills us up!

"Okay. You can now open your eyes!" Mom says.

I'm standing in front of a giant mound of Christmas presents.

These are all mine!

My siblings have just as many. Between our three piles, colorfully wrapped boxes tied in red and green ribbon cover the entire floor.

"Yay!" I scream.

The three of us start ripping into the gifts, giggling and laughing the entire time.

"Look what I got!" Ralph exclaims. "A new truck!"

"I got a Barbie camper!" I scream. "Oh, my gosh!"

Wrapping paper flies everywhere. For once, Mom doesn't care that things aren't orderly. Our collective happiness and excitement consumes us all.

CHAPTER 4

Controlling Mom

I WISH THOSE CAREFREE, HAPPY FAMILY moments lasted all year long, but they don't.

I wake to the sound of Dad's brown Mitsubishi diesel truck fading away as he drives down the street headed for work. The morning breeze flows through the open windows in my bedroom. I love the smell of morning. I open my eyes and exhale. It's summertime and I don't have to go to school.

Suddenly the door to the bedroom flies open. My entire body tenses.

"Get up!" my mother yells. "You're not going to sleep all day!"

Moments later I hear her repeat the same thing to my brother. I climb out of bed and open my closet to get dressed. There they are. My favorite pretty pastel-pink pants. I wish I could wear them with the matching pink striped top, but they aren't play clothes and Mom would disapprove. So instead I slide into my ratty old jean shorts, old T-shirt and Nikes. Fortunately, I don't have to bathe this morning because we already had our regimented nightly bath last night. Mine occurs promptly at 7:00 p.m.

I turn to my bed. If I had it my way, I would pull the bedspread up to the pillow and just be done, but making our beds correctly is a big deal in our house. I know what's expected of me. I pull up the bottom sheet as tightly as possible and then pull up the blanket and bedspread tightly as well. I grab a clothes hanger and gently glide it from the top to the bottom of the red bedspread to get out any of the remaining wrinkles. Our beds must have no creases, and I don't want Mom to get mad. God help me if I incur her wrath yet again when she is in control mode. I fear she'll yank off all my bed linens and throw them on the floor just like she did last week when I did not make the bed properly.

"You will learn how to make a bed, young lady, if you have to make it ten times," she yelled.

You're such an idiot, I told myself again and again as I re-made my bed, crying the entire time.

Even as I said the words, I thought, *What has happened to my loving mom?* Looking back now, I realize that the stress of having two more kids in the house triggered her behavior to change. At the time, all I saw was a cruel and controlling mother who by the time I was just seven years old was totally foreign to me.

Like good little soldiers, we all march downstairs because we don't want to be late for breakfast. I take my seat at the table lined with three bowls of Cheerios. It's always Cheerios. We each have the same bowl of Cheerios and a small glass of orange juice as we do every day without exception. Just once I would love to have Fruit Loops, or even just a piece of toast for variety.

Don't think about it, Michelle. It's never going to happen, I say to myself.

As we eat breakfast I study Mom to see how she is today. I need to get a good enough read on her to anticipate how the day will go. I don't want to seem like I'm in a good mood or happy because that can get her mad as well.

She seems agitated—I'd better watch it! I think to myself.

Mom comes back into the kitchen just as we're finishing our breakfast. We quickly hush our breakfast conversation as if our talking at the breakfast table is illegal. She doesn't say anything and collects our bowls. My sister heads upstairs to the bathroom, as she does every day, to "set our toothbrushes." She is trained to do this after every meal. She sets our three toothbrushes neatly with one line of toothpaste each and then lines up the three toothbrushes in a row. Mom doesn't trust Ralph or me to do this task neatly. We're too young. When Mary comes downstairs, my brother goes upstairs to brush his teeth. Today he is taking too long. Mom hollers upstairs, "Ralph, hurry up! What are you doing up there?" He comes rushing downstairs and I run upstairs. I have to hurry, or I will get yelled at, too.

When I'm done, I immediately start emptying and cleaning all the ashtrays in the house.

I hate doing this! I say to myself.

The ashtrays are always overfilled, and they smell horrible and filthy! They are piled high with cigarette butts and smell like stale smoke. If I'm not careful, the dust will go everywhere, including in my face. I tip them into the trash slowly and gently. As I wash them in the kitchen sink, thick black liquid comes off them.

Yuck, I think. There are four ashtrays upstairs and another four downstairs that all must be emptied and cleaned. *Why do they have to smoke so much?*

Changing the three hand towels in the kitchen is an easy chore compared with emptying and cleaning out those nasty ashtrays!

My brother has to deal with the ashes, too, because his chores include collecting and emptying all the trash cans in the house.

My sister's chores are doing laundry and washing dishes after dinner. She gets the laundry from the hamper in the hallway. I watch her as she carries the brimming laundry basket to the basement. I see her struggling, so without saying anything I grab a pile of clothes to help her get down the stairs. She separates the mountain of laundry. The piles and piles of different colored clothes spread out across the basement floor represent one week's worth of laundry for five people.

We go upstairs once the wash has been started, pleased to have finished our chores.

Mom lights a cigarette.

"Outside!" she commands. "Go play in the yard and get out of my hair!"

We are not in the yard for just a few hours. We are out there until late afternoon.

It's going to be a long day! I say to myself.

I can tell it's going to be hot out by how the morning air feels. We are only allowed to play in the backyard and with one another. We are not allowed to go out into the front unless we asked permission which stinks because we like playing with Robbie, Jennifer, Carrie, Lisa and Danny who all live just across the street. Mary is the only one freely allowed inside the house throughout the day because she still has to contend with the piles of laundry. If my brother and I want to go inside the house to use the bathroom, we have to ring the bell and ask Mom for permission.

At home we have to ask permission for everything we want to do, all of the time. We even have to ask permission to get a drink of water and to be excused from the table. We also have to ask permission to play with a craft set or a game from the playroom. And forget about turning the channel when it's TV time. That is never allowed.

Mom has us well disciplined and trained. She controls everything, even the air that we breathe. Literally.

On our way home from a family shopping trip at Sears, Mom and Dad both light up before we reach the car in the parking lot. We pile into the back seat of the red family Mercury Marquis. Mom takes a drag on her cigarette and coughs. As we leave the store parking lot, smoke is already filling up the car and the air vents are pushing the smoke to the back seat. It's getting hard to breathe and I'm starting to get nauseated. I'm used to being around smoke, but this is a lot of smoke for such a cramped space.

"Can you please open the window?" I ask Dad. "I can't breathe."

Dad cracks the window a half of an inch. It doesn't help. There is just too much smoke for that small of an opening. I lean forward to try to get some of the air coming in from the window. My eyes are now burning. I try asking Mom.

"Mom, can you please open the window some more?"

I feel like a fish trying to suck in the little bit of air from the tiny crack in the window.

"It's already open," she snaps.

Her tone tells me all that I need to know. The conversation has come to an end. I know better than to challenge her.

Just as I don't protest the lack of oxygen in the car, I don't ever question the mandate to be in our backyard. Now, our backyard is fairly good-sized, with a red rectangular picnic table, an above-ground pool with a deck, a jungle gym and a small sand-box with a canopy. On the other side of the pool there is a small vegetable garden where Dad grows tomatoes, peppers and a few other vegetables. Regardless, it's not a place I enjoy spending end-less hours in, especially on days like today when it's 90 degrees. It's just too hot. Even though two large trees in one section of our yard afford some shade during certain points in the day, it's not nearly enough.

At first, being confined to the backyard doesn't seem that bad. I start picking long strands of grass and searching for the right-sized twigs so that I can weave them together.

I can make a cute little nature gift, I think.

There are many natural toys back here in the yard, so I have fun for a short while. Before long, however, I start getting really hot and bored with my nature crafts. My forehead is covered in beads of sweat because it's too early in the day for the canopy of branches from our big oak trees to provide any shade. I look over to the turquoise-blue water of our pool that sparkles in the sunlight. I just want to jump in and cool off, but I can't. I know the rules. I can't go in the pool until Mom comes out later this afternoon. Even that is no guarantee. Some days she just watches soap operas in the air conditioning all afternoon.

"Please let her come out this afternoon," I pray in a low voice.

Even if she does, I still have a few more hours to keep myself busy and try somehow to stay cool. That isn't easy. Mom is al-ways watching us from the kitchen window. She sees everything we do. When she isn't looking for a quick moment, I dip my hands in the pool and rinse my sweaty forehead with the cool chlorine water. I don't get caught, but I don't dare push my luck and do it again.

Now what?

My brother is playing with his Matchbox cars in the dirt under the deck where it's cool, but there are lots of spiders and other bugs under there. So despite being hot and bored, I don't join him. Instead, I climb on the jungle gym and sit on the top bars. I feel so tall! I'm so high up that I can see clear over our stockade fence onto the cars driving down West Broad Street. I can see into our neighbors' yards and even clear down the street. However, the monkey bars are quite hot and sitting up there is making me even hotter. I come down quickly from my perch in search of some relief.

In the corner of the yard behind the garage, I notice all the weeds. Mom told us to pull them today while we were in the backyard, but I don't want to.

I hate those ugly weeds, I say to myself. *They smell funny.*

That's not the only problem. The weeds, which have bamboo-like stalks and wide green leaves, have grown taller than me. Mom made us pull some of them just two weeks ago. I still have the mosquito bites on my legs from being in that dense patch of weeds. After pulling and pulling those weeds, my hands and fingernails had become stained with green. It's like I never pulled any weeds at all. Worse, they seem to just multiply. I can't even see the ground because they've grown so thick. No wonder they intimidate me. It's like they're taking over.

I can't stand the thought of getting all sweaty and covered in green, dirt and mosquitoes again like my friend Katie and I experienced just a few short weeks ago.

Just pretend you never heard her ask us to weed, I say to myself.

Instead I walk over to the picnic table to see if my crayon pieces have melted on the plate in the sunlight to form that colorful kaleidoscope I like to create.

"Mary, come and get the lunch tray," Mom yells out the window.

My sister heads into the house to get our food.

I hope we're having PB&J today!

I just love PB&J. Even though it's never PB&J, for some reason I still hope that just this one time it might be. I know better than to ask for what I really want.

We open the gate for Mary, and she sets the giant green tray on the picnic table. No PB&J today. Instead, there they are. Three sandwich plates on the tray with three tomato sandwiches on white bread lathered with a thick layer of mayonnaise. Same as every single day during summer, even though we hate them. This is actually the best of the bad lunch options. During the school year, we would take our lunch to school only to find olive loaf or pimento loaf sandwiches on white bread that we loathed as well. At least in school we could easily toss our sandwiches and use the spare change we gathered at home to buy something we actually wanted to eat from the cafeteria. But this is not the case at home. There is no way we can return those plates with anything on them. Mom will scrutinize them to make sure we have consumed all the sandwiches. There is no escape; even Teddy does not eat tomato sandwiches. We have to eat them. So there we sit in the sunlight, forcing down our mushy tomato sandwiches.

By the time we finish eating, the three tall, beige Tupperware cups of milk at the center of the sandwich tray have gotten warm from the sun. Just like every meal, we aren't allowed to drink anything until we finish eating. Cold milk is great. This milk is not. We drink it anyway, afraid not to.

My sister returns the empty tray to the kitchen and gets to stay inside in the cool basement doing the laundry. My brother and I do our best to occupy ourselves and keep cool during what is now the hottest part of the day.

I really hope we can go swimming today, I think for the one thousandth time.

If Mom is in a good mood today, she might come outside and go onto the deck of our above-ground pool. If she does, she might allow us to swim for a few hours while she reclines and naps in her lounge chair.

Please let her be in a good mood today.

Mom emerges in the middle of the afternoon in her bathing suit, her towel in hand. She climbs up the stairs onto the deck.

"Well, do you want to go swimming?" she asks. "Then go inside and put on your bathing suit. You have five minutes."

We scramble inside the house. I gobble down some water on the way through the kitchen. I'm so thirsty from the heat outside that I can't get enough. I don't even try. We're lucky that we're going to be able to swim and enjoy the pool for the rest of the afternoon. I don't want to push my luck.

Our window of fun in the sun comes to an end way too soon.

"Out of the pool," Mom says. "Now!"

Her relaxed mood has flipped. We can sense her stress of having to fix dinner.

Oh, no, I say to myself. She must have just realized the time and that Dad will be home soon. *Hurry, hurry, hurry.*

I dry off just enough to get to the basement, where I strip off my wet bathing suit and put on my freshly washed and folded clothes. I rush upstairs, collect the silverware and plates, and head to the dining room table.

Oh, crap! What side of the plate does the knife go on? I ask myself. *I've got to get this right!*

I don't want to goof. She doesn't like it when I goof. I finish setting the table and she comes to look at it.

Whew, I got it right this time. Thank God!

Last week I wasn't so lucky. I goofed setting the table.

"How old are you?" she yelled at me. "Jesus, Michelle, you're seven years old now and you still don't know how to set a table? When are you going to get it through your thick head how to set a table properly?"

She glared at me with disgust, her face contorting and her nostrils flaring. "Michelle, you are so stupid!" she concludes. Again.

How could you get this wrong? I think. *You idiot!*

In that moment, I hate my stupid self and I hate my life. Upsetting my mother is the worst possible thing that anyone could do.

Dad arrives home from work and we all sit quietly while Mom puts dinner on the table. Tonight, we're having meatloaf and boiled lima beans. I hate lima beans. I can't even stand the smell of them.

The feeling of rigidness lasts the whole meal. When we're finished eating, I collect the plates and glasses and bring them to the kitchen. Typically, Mary will wash the dishes, and I will dry them and put them away. Some nights, like tonight, when my sister is babysitting two kids down the street, I have to wash the dishes as well. I'm standing at the kitchen sink washing dishes when Mom comes over to the counter next to me. Luckily, her mood has suddenly improved, so she doesn't check my work. That wasn't the case last week.

"Missy, you call this clean?" she yelled. "This pot is far from clean, young lady! Wash it again."

The irony is that a month later that very same pot, badly burnt with tomato sauce, will sit in the sink full of dirty dishes for days. The kitchen counter, crusted over with old food and crumbs, will also sit there untouched until either my father or one of us kids decides to clean it up. And Mom won't say a word. She won't even notice.

After all the dishes are put away and the kitchen is cleaned up for the night, we march upstairs for our baths and tooth-brushing. Then we head into the television room, where my parents are relaxing in their recliners.

I hope I get the big pillow tonight, I think.

I don't want to sit on the cold floor with the thin pillow. We gather our pillows and grab a space to watch television together. *The Muppet Show* is on. I love the Muppets! For the next thirty minutes, I'm able to temporarily forget what my home life is like.

CHAPTER 5

School Break

WHEN MOM IS IN HER CONTROLLING STATE, she's strict, her expectations are high, and the repercussions are significant. Everything must be done at a certain time and in a special way. Home is a lot like a prison where you have to follow the rules just to cope.

At least when school is in session, I get a little breather from Mom and her controlling ways. In the morning before school, I eat my cereal with a sense of possibility for what the day will hold because I'm breaking out. I don't have to deal with the rules or the confines of this house for the day.

After breakfast I walk to school, leaving no later than 8:15 a.m. so that I have enough time to walk across town. School is a welcome change. Even though the academics are challenging and getting good grades is hard for me because I have a tough time concentrating, I really appreciate the social aspect.

As I walk through the hallway at school, I feel happy and a little relieved to be there.

"Hi, Michelle," Sarah says.

"Hey, Michelle," Kevin hollers.

"What's up, Michelle?" Tanya says.

I have so many friends and as they all call out to me, for a brief moment I feel popular, acknowledged and accepted. At school my presence matters.

I run up to my friend Robyn, who's at her locker.

"Hey, Robyn. How's it going?"

She smiles back at me.

In that moment I forget about Mom. That's not always the case, but I never let on when I'm upset. Instead, I put on my happy face and try hard to be that funny girl. Getting someone to laugh makes me feel good inside and temporarily allows me to step away from my emotionally draining home environment. Besides, when I'm funny and charismatic, the other kids gravitate toward me. I can't get enough of that positive attention. I sure don't get it at home, especially when Mom is in her controlling—or worse, abusive—state.

CHAPTER 6

Abusive Mom

ALL TOO OFTEN, CONTROLLING MOM morphs into abusive Mom, a tendency that began with the arrival of my siblings. My mom is out to raise perfectly disciplined little soldiers. Her face lights up when someone compliments her on our behavior in public. It's like she is in competition with herself to be the best mother ever. For her, being a good mother means that your kids are under control and well behaved. And, she is willing to do whatever it takes to make sure her kids turn out okay.

Unfortunately, this makes it really hard to be a kid in our house. Disobeying the rules and back talking are the two things that set Mom off. That can result in being thrown clear across the room, slapped across the face or having a wooden spoon broken on you. I've stopped counting how many wooden spoons have been broken in our house.

One pivotal episode still remains with me. It's the yardstick that I compare every future spanking with. For while the physical abuse really hurts, the emotional abuse inflicted on my four-year-old self would ultimately dictate my sense of self-worth as a teenager and as an adult.

"Michelle, it's time for your nap," Mom hollers downstairs to me from the upstairs banister. "Okay," I respond, as I fix my Toughskin jeans. Today I'm looking forward to my nap. When Mom was in the shower, I snuck downstairs and took a jumbo pack of orange-flavored Trident gum and tucked it into my pocket! I love chewing gum, but Mom only lets us have it on certain occasions. She tightly controls everything in our house.

I hustle upstairs to my bedroom and climb into my bed. Mom tucks in my blanket and leaves, closing the bedroom door behind her.

Ah-ha, she's gone now, I think.

I pull the blanket up over my head. Quietly, I open the pack of gum and start unwrapping several pieces. I proceed to stuff as many pieces of juicy and delicious gum into my mouth as I can. It's so yummy and sweet! I can't seem to chew fast enough to get all the orange flavor out. This is the best naptime ever!

Suddenly, the bedroom door swings open. It's Mom! Oh, no! I break into a cold sweat. I can already feel it. I am going to be in unimaginable trouble this time.

Mom whips back the blanket from over my head. There it is—a pile of orange gum paper wrappings and the remaining half a pack of gum. Half the evidence is there in plain sight. My mouth is stuffed with the rest of it like a chipmunk. There's so much gum in my cheeks that I can hardly talk.

"Spit it out!" Mom yells at me as she puts her hand in front of my mouth. "You thief!"

She is so angry that her face is red and her lip is twitching. The whites of her eyes make it look like her eyeballs are about to pop out of her head.

"You stole that gum out of the kitchen drawer. Who the hell do you think you are? We steal now in this house? Who taught you to steal? Are you proud of yourself, young lady?"

She draws her hand back to above her shoulder and strikes me across the face with her hand over and over and over again.

With every slap my skin stings more and more, and the disappointment of letting her down causes me to cry harder with each blow.

"Stop crying!" she yells. "Or I will really give you something to cry about!"

I can't stop crying and I don't know how she expects me to. It hurts so badly. On top of that, her anger and disappointment overwhelm me with shame.

It's now getting hard to breathe because I'm crying so hard. That only encourages her to keep hitting. I have never seen Mom this mad. She seems to be in a trance-like state. It's almost like she is enjoying a release of pent-up rage.

I can't believe she is still hitting me. How long will she keep going?

I am sweating now, and my face is starting to feel numb from her hand repeatedly slapping my skin.

She has to stop soon. Please make it end.

Finally, after what seems like an hour, the beating subsides, and she storms out of my bedroom and slams the bedroom door with all her might. The door crashes shut, making me jump.

Alone, I wonder why I ever thought that stealing that gum was a good idea. Stupid, stupid me. Somehow, Mom always finds out when I do something wrong. I don't know why I even try to get away with anything. I know that when I'm caught the repercussions will be horrible. Today is the all-time worst day.

Ten minutes go by and I still can't stop shaking. I clutch my teddy bear and burrow beneath the covers as I continue to cry and shake. I hate her right now. I hate that she is my mother and I hate this life. It's so unfair. Why was I adopted? Why couldn't I have stayed with my real family? I should not be here. There has been a horrible mistake and I really don't belong here.

The abuse that begins when I'm just four years old does not let up. And it's not just physical. Especially when I became a mouthy adolescent. And if I'm stupid enough to respond poorly, I get the crap beaten out of me no matter how old I am.

"Don't you dare disrespect me, young lady," Mom yells at me as I put my coat on and head out the door. "How dare you!"

This reaction is not unusual. How I respond is so important. Even though I think I've developed a shell to protect against her sharp and abrasive words, somehow they always seem to reach me at my core. That verbal and emotional abuse always seems to sting more than the pain of the physical abuse.

The mood is set in our house daily by whether you are the one on the shit list. Yesterday, my sister was on the shit list and I was thankful it wasn't me.

"Mary, I told you to not mix the whites with the colored laundry. Are you an idiot?"

No matter what she did, it was wrong, and she was hit and ridiculed verbally.

"How many times do I have to tell you the same thing?" Mom asked as she slapped Mary's face over and over again in the kitchen.

I didn't want to see it. I scurried away to my room to avoid witnessing any more hitting.

This scene is repeated weekly. Days when I am not on the shit list are better for me because I know it means that for a day I'll escape being yelled at or smacked. Mom having her sights on someone else means a brief reprieve for my other sibling and me.

That reprieve is always short lived. Two days ago, I watched my brother be on the shit list and get the crap beat out of him for not cleaning up his room. He talked back to Mom, which only fuels her rage. She hit him so hard with the wooden spoon that it broke clear in half. Having then witnessed my sister's beating yesterday, I'm dreading today. I know she'll be coming for me. I know that today I won't be able to do anything right, no matter how hard I try.

Sure enough, it's like she awakened mad at me and I don't know why. I need to lie low, do exactly what I'm told and pray that I won't get it as bad as they did.

I tiptoe into the kitchen to get a glass of water, thinking that Mom is in the basement doing laundry. She grabs me by the back of my hair and slaps me across the face.

"Why did you leave your filthy backpack on the kitchen table? I told you not to!" she yells.

Why did I go into the kitchen?

We all have left our backpacks on the kitchen table, but today I'm the target for not following the rules. It sucks.

Even when we're not being physically abused, more often than not my siblings and I are made to feel completely insignificant. Mom makes it painfully obvious that she's in control and that we don't matter.

"I don't give a crap about what you want. I don't give a crap about what you need," she regularly tells us. "You're going to do what I say to do whether you like it or not."

When I drop or break something, I hear a different version of being worthless.

"You're careless and stupid!" she screams. "How can you be so clumsy, you dummy?"

We're constantly being torn down and ripped apart.

"You're a good-for-nothing snot brat kid. You're so dumb."

Unfortunately, those statements become our own internal dialogue and impact how we view ourselves all the time.

As my brother and sister and I all grow up together, the abuse along with general conditions on the home front get worse. I can tell that Mary, now a teenager, is not happy. Mom makes her do a lot of the household chores. She's not very nice to her, either, forcing her to wear hand-me-down clothes from my nana, who is now in her seventies. I know how much Mary hates that, because she's totally embarrassed when her friends see her.

At 1:00 one morning, I awake to the sound of our bedroom floor creaking as my sister slowly creeps toward the door of our bedroom.

"Go back to sleep," she whispers to me.

She has to sneak out of bed during the middle of the night to wash her hair in the basement sink. She does this every couple of days because Mom forbids her from washing her hair more than once a week. Most nights she is quiet enough, so nobody hears her. Some nights she is not so lucky. Ultimately, this is a no-win situation. Even if she does not get caught at night, she gets caught in the morning because Mom always finds her wet hair towels.

Punishment for infractions seems even more severe for Mary than for Ralph and me, perhaps because she's older. When she cut school with her girlfriend once, Mom went looking for her. By the time she caught the two of them in the Hanes parking lot, she was furious. That beating, with my sister crying hysterically, still plays in my head. I hated hearing every minute of that, and thirty-five years later, I hate the mental replay.

That physical abuse proves to be the tipping point for my sister. A few weeks later, seven or so years after arriving at our house as a ten-year-old, she runs away from home. A week later and much to her dismay, the Division of Youth and Family Services (DYFS) brings her back home to us.

I'm thrilled to see my sister at home again, but Mary is clearly not happy and doesn't want to stay here anymore. To my chagrin, she even changes toward me. She no longer wants to make me smile and laugh. She becomes distant, which confuses me and makes me sad. Eventually she runs away yet again, this time for good, and moves into her best friend's house.

My sister's departure triggers my mother even more. She eventually redirects her focus onto my brother. At a time when Ralph is dealing with his sister abandoning him, he suddenly must endure even more physical and emotional abuse from my mother.

"Ralph, you an idiot? What is wrong with you?" she screams at him. "You must be retarded."

Even worse are the beatings that follow when she gets really mad. She slaps him with her hand several times in the face or beats him with a wooden spoon or belt.

Unfortunately, Ralph, who is now fourteen years old, always makes the mistake of talking back to Mom. It's like he can't help himself.

"What did you say to me?" she screams in his face. "Say it again!"

He says nothing. At this point she has him cornered by the kitchen sink. She starts hitting him with the wooden spoon in her hand.

"I asked you what you said," she shouts. "Do you think you're funny?"

After what seems like forever, the wooden spoon finally snaps, and the handle goes flying across the kitchen counter. So many wooden spoons have been broken in that kitchen. Thankfully, this beating comes to an end.

I can overhear the beatings and I hate hearing Ralph cry when he finally gets to go back to his room, which is right across the hall from mine. Most of the time I have no idea what he did wrong that caused her to get so angry.

Beatings like the one this afternoon are not isolated incidents. He's lucky if this only happens once a day. When I hear Mom lay into him, for a brief moment a sense of relief sweeps over me. This time it's not me who's getting it. But another part of me is consumed with sadness for the pain that he's being put through. It's not fair. Ralph has lost his father and his mother, and now his sister. He has to deal with this all by himself and I can't help him.

Shortly thereafter, the physical abuse becomes just too much for Ralph to bear. Just a few short months after Mary's departure, I come home from school and he's not there. His room is a mess and I can tell that most of his personal things are gone. Just this morning, he'd been crying because Mom was pounding on him. I understand why he has left. Sometimes I wish I could go, too. I speculate that my brother and sister are together someplace else where they won't be beaten all the time.

At home I can't ask Mom or Dad any questions about them being gone or why they left. It's understood that this is not to be discussed. And I know better than to push back. Mom refuses to acknowledge how sad we all are because they are both gone. Feelings and emotions are suppressed, swept under the carpet and never dealt with. When the story later emerges, my parents react with great anger and discontent, focusing on my siblings' ingratitude for all that was done for them.

Part of me resists believing that my siblings have left forever. I fantasize about them coming home and things reverting to the way they were when they first came to live with us—a relatively happy family of five. But months go by and they never return home.

Deep down inside, I struggle to understand it all. I know that Mom doesn't really intend to be cruel. She only gets abusive because she is not well. I want to believe that my sister and brother love me, and that we will be a family again one day. I really don't understand how they can just leave me behind.

I know one thing for sure. Mom has caused everything to shift and for them to leave. It's Mom's fault that I'm alone here once again.

Even once the pressures and stress of housing two extra kids have lifted, Mom doesn't return to the way she was before their arrival. Confronted by the evidence that she has failed as a mother, she's increasingly more irritable. And now she has nobody else to pick on but me. The abuse escalates.

One afternoon the doorbell rings. Mom greets two people wearing suits at the front door and lets them in. Rather than talking to them nicely, as she would if it were her friends, she seems annoyed.

"She's right there," Mom says brusquely, pointing to me.

Then her voice changes to one I barely recognize.

"Sweetie, come here and show these nice people that you're fine."

"Hi!" I say to the nice people.

They look me over and seem satisfied with what they see. Moments later they leave, and Mom gets on the phone. I overhear her conversation.

"The Division of Youth and Family Services was here to see if I know how to be a parent," Mom says into the phone. "I don't know just who the hell they think they are! We provided a damn good home for those kids!"

I can tell by how she is talking that she is extremely angry. I dart off to my room.

Over the next several months, DYFS returns to evaluate the circumstances in an attempt to understand why two children would want to run away and never come back. The unannounced visits, along with the interrogation of my mother and father's parenting skills, infuriate Mom. When the DYFS people finally leave, she lashes out. I do my best to lie low.

Then one morning, everything changes. Mom is not herself. She doesn't wake me up in her usual manner, and my cereal bowl isn't set and waiting for me at the table. Those are my cues. I know what this means. I know that she is about to get sick again. In just a matter of months, our house will go from pristinely organized to cluttered and completely filthy.

I can't wait.

CHAPTER 7

Tears

MOM HAS BEEN SICK FOR THE PAST few weeks. Our house has slipped from control into complete chaos, and I have moved from a sense of relief to a sense of burden.

When Mom begins her downward slide, I feel unfettered. For a brief moment, she isn't watching my every move waiting for me to mess up so she can hit me. I can breathe again and actually live my life.

This freedom is short-lived. Before I know it, there is a new role for me to play.

Morning comes, and I cannot wait to escape to school. It's mentally and emotionally draining to be trapped in a house with someone who is always crying. Besides, I don't get to hang out with my friends nearly enough since they never come over and I have to be here so much.

Today I have a brand-new cute outfit to wear—a pink and white fuzzy sweater with a pink jean miniskirt. I just love wearing pink. I've got my whole look planned out. In my hair I'm going to wear my favorite pink and white braided barrettes embellished with white beads on the bottom. Finally, I'm going to look as good as the other seventh-graders. I can't wait to see the reaction of the kids in my class.

I look at the clock. I have to hurry. I'm meeting my friend Katie, so that we can walk to school together. I want to get there early so I can see Wesley, a new boy who likes me.

I get dressed and go downstairs. Immediately, I can tell that Mom is in an even darker place. While her moods have been erratic lately, I didn't really think much about it until now. I should have been paying more attention. I should have seen this coming!

As I think back, I realize that during the day when she's not crying, she has been rushing around the house at an incredibly fast pace. She has also kept herself super-busy doing small tasks like organizing the catch-all drawer in the kitchen for hours and hours on end. She cries at night instead of sleeping, unless she's on a tear with a project. When I get up to use the bathroom, she is downstairs in the living room with all the lights on, wide awake, crocheting or doing needlepoint. At the time, I wonder how she can go so many nights without sleeping. Now I know.

This morning the large red bags below her bloodshot eyes confirm for me that she has been up all night again. No crafts this time. She obviously cried the whole time. The pure sadness on her face overwhelms me.

Oh, crap! Not again! I say to myself with a sigh. *We're heading down that dark road again.*

I try to ignore the all-too-familiar sense of despair and go about my morning routine. As I make my bowl of cereal for breakfast, I overhear my parents' conversation.

"Please stay home with me," Mom begs my dad with a whimper.

"I can't stay home today—period," Dad replies. "I have a very busy schedule and an important meeting with my boss."

"Please," she says as she starts to cry. "I don't want to be all alone."

Dad reluctantly turns to me. He has no other option at this point.

"Do you want to stay home with your mother today?" he asks.

I'm already showered and dressed for school. I want to see my friends. I want to see the new boy. I even want to go to class. The one thing I positively don't want to do is stay here with my crying mother.

"Yes, I can stay home," I say as I think about all that I will miss in school, including that assembly that I was really looking forward to. None of that matters. Mom needs me now and her needs come first.

"Michelle will stay home with you today," Dad announces to Mom as I unpack my lunch and put it back into the refrigerator.

Staying home for most kids is a gift. It's not that for me. I know what this means, and I know what is coming.

The last time this happened, I stayed home for almost a week with Mom. Dad went off to work, leaving me to deal with her imbalance and try everything in my power to reverse her symptoms. I just wanted to stop her sadness. I knew that if I just tried harder this time, I would be able to help her. But the harder I tried, the worse she got. As always, when she hit rock bottom she was taken away to the hospital.

My inability to make her better makes me feel like a failure.

During the slow depression she's in right now, she starts the morning in the same chair in the living room wearing her red silk pajamas that she will stay in for most of the day. The living room is dark, with just a small sunbeam spilling through the wooden shutters. The cigarette smoke forges a visible cloud in the sunlight. She calls on me to refill her coffee cup multiple times and to empty her ashtray as she lights cigarette after cigarette. Her hands shake each time she picks up the cigarette and lifts it to her lips. Her nerves are totally shot again.

I don't even try to talk to her. When she is like this and I try to talk to her, she gives me short one-word answers, or she shakes her head and doesn't answer me at all. I get the sense that in some way she is trying to shield me from knowing how she is really feeling, but I can tell without her saying a word.

Once Dad leaves for work, Mom makes her way upstairs to the small TV room in the rear corner of the second floor, where she remains for the rest of the day. With just enough space for two recliners and a small television, there is barely room for Dad's IBM computer and paper-fed dot matrix printer tucked into the far corner of the room. The space feels dirty and smells like burnt cigarettes due to the overflowing ashtrays on the end tables adjacent to each recliner. As the cloud of cigarette smoke spills out into the hallway, Mom lies in her recliner watching morning talk shows and game shows while drifting in and out of a light sleep.

I take advantage of her dozing to look out the window at the oak tree leaves dancing in the wind against a pristine blue sky. The tree seems so vibrant and alive. I watch a small squirrel dart from branch to branch and hear a bird singing so sweetly. Out there, the tree encapsulates life within its branches. In here, it's anything but that.

I think about where I would be if I were in school right now. Third period is about to end. I would be getting ready for my art class. I love art class. After that I would see my girlfriends at lunch.

Mom's sadness feels heavy on me and in turn I feel myself becoming sad. My mind drifts off as I wonder if my friends are asking where I am. I also think about what I could be missing in my classes. I know that I'm missing a big math test today. I'd felt relieved about that earlier in the day, but now reality has set in. How am I going to make up that test? This grade accounts for a large percentage of my grade.

Oh, shoot, I just wish I could have gone to school today, I say to myself. *Why does Mom have to be sick? Again.*

When *The Price Is Right* begins, I know what this means. Mom gets up from her chair and puts on old dirty clothes hanging on the hallway banister. Then off we go. I know where we're headed.

We return from our fast-food run and proceed straight back to the TV room, where we sit with our meals. Mom is in her recliner indulging in her Big Mac, large french fries and chocolate shake. I've got my Happy Meal, which on this day seems utterly misnamed. Mom tops off her lunch with a slice of chocolate cake for dessert. I can see that her addiction to food and sugar is her way of self-medicating the depression. It seems to soothe and even numb her to the point that her mood temporarily eases.

Mom's mood impacts me more than I like to believe. As I watch her fade into the stories of her soap operas, I feel more and more alone. I, too, slip away and lose myself in that fantasy world. *The Young and the Restless* has always been one of my favorite shows. You can see how much in love Nikki and Victor are with each other. I love watching their romantic kisses. I envision a happier life just like Nikki's when I grow up. I imagine the closeness they share. That escape is a welcomed distraction.

Mom rarely makes it through a whole show. Each time she wakes up after a short nap, she begins crying again. My presence seems to make no difference to her. It's like I'm not even there. Anything that's bothering me is not only insignificant, it's not even a part of the equation.

The reality of my role sets in. My presence is really a command performance. I'm just supposed to be with her today without expecting anything in return. Mom is too consumed by her own mind for there to be any room for me. There seems no way to pull her out of her misery. All I can do is sit here.

Eventually I attempt to talk to her anyway. I can't give up. I have to try something to make her feel better.

"Mom, did I tell you that my friends really liked my hand-made braided barrettes?"

"Uh huh," she mumbles, rolling over on her other side in her recliner so that her back is to me.

She clearly has no interest in talking to me. This is not the mom who wants to know all about how I am and what is going on with me with school or with my friends. This is the mom who through her own illness forces me to become her mother rather than the other way around.

I wander downstairs and get her a fresh glass of iced tea. I bring it up to her and put it down on the glass-covered end table next to her chair. She looks at me and doesn't respond. As I pick up candy wrappers and empty her ashtray, she rolls over to her other side as if to avoid looking at my face. This has happened before. Many times. And each time I feel rejected.

A short while later, she wakes and begins sobbing. I don't understand why. I never understand why. Again, I try to get her to talk with me, but she remains uninterested. Why can't I reach her? If I could only get her to talk to me, I know I could pull her out of her depression and get my loving and caring mom back.

As she escapes into a fantasy world of afternoon soap operas, I come to terms with what I know is going to happen next. Things will escalate and ultimately take a turn for the worse. I just have to try to make the best of a bad situation.

I've gotten good at that. I force myself to stop thinking about what I'm missing at school today. I force myself to stop thinking about what's about to happen to Mom. But while I may be able to control my thoughts, I can't escape my feelings.

I feel Mom's sadness like a thick, heavy blanket on top of me, suffocating me. As always, her feelings become my feelings. If there is sadness or chaos at home, that is how I feel. If there is depression at home, that is how I feel. I have to feel that way, too, because the mood of the day engulfs me. Instead of feeling my own emotions, I just absorb hers.

When I finally can break free long enough to gauge my own emotional state, I realize that I am stuck in a situation I can't escape. I'm trapped. My needs are insignificant and don't matter, just like me. I'm invisible.

CHAPTER 8

Substitute Moms

I'M NOT JUST INVISIBLE AT HOME. Caring for Mom and missing school for long stretches at a time causes me to live in isolation, making it hard for me to reintegrate into school or to make and maintain friendships. In some ways it's easier to be confined to my house, especially since I've just returned to public school after being in Catholic school.

Having to meet new kids and make new friends isn't easy, but Mr. Harrison has a way of making it okay by including me and having me feel a part of the class. Months later, a new student joins our class. Robyn, who has moved here from North Jersey, is very pretty with her long brown hair and vibrant smile. I'm put in charge of helping her get settled, as Mr. Harrison calls it. I don't mind because I know how she must feel, especially since she's shy and quiet. Before long, we become friends.

One day after school, I get to meet Robyn's mom when she comes to pick up Robyn. She's immediately friendly, as if I have met her before.

"Hi, sweetie," she says to me. "I'm Mom Colucci. I've heard a lot about you from Robyn. Do you need a ride home from school, too?"

"No, I'm okay. I live in that red house just down the street," I say, pointing to my house.

"Would you like to come over this weekend?" she asks. "You could play at our house and have pizza with us."

"Really? That would be so much fun!" I exclaim. "I'll run home and ask my mom right away. Thank you!"

I can't wait to get home and ask for permission. I can just tell it's going to be fun! Excited, I launch into a discourse about being invited to their house. I haven't even finished before Mom interrupts me.

"That Robyn is spoiled."

"Really?" I respond. "She doesn't seem spoiled to me and her mom was super-nice."

"You can go on Saturday, but she *is* spoiled. Just because she gets whatever she wants, don't think you'll be getting the same."

"Okay," I say, not really knowing what that all means. I guess Mom doesn't like Robyn or her mother, but I think they're both nice and I like how I feel when I'm around them.

Saturday finally arrives, and I'm beyond excited. As soon as Mom drops me off, this carefree feeling comes over me. I have temporarily left all the rigid rules and expectations behind me.

Robyn answers the door and I go inside. Their house just feels different. It's not perfectly organized. The kitchen table has a bunch of papers on it and there are clothes in the hallway. Yet, just being there makes me feel warm and relaxed.

From the moment I walk into the house, I immediately pick up on laughter and a fun energy that doesn't ever make an appearance at our address.

"Hi, Michelle," Bob, Robyn's stepfather, says with an open smile. "How are you doing?"

"I'm good," I respond.

We head to Robyn's room to play with our hair and makeup. Her entire vanity is filled with girlie things like makeup, ribbons and barrettes. As we braid our hair, we chitchat about boys and school. Moments later, Robyn's mom enters her bedroom. She's very sweet and pretty, with long dark hair and skin like a china doll. She's so pretty that some of the boys in our class have made comments about her beauty—and she's a mother! She gives me a hug hello and I immediately feel welcomed and so comfortable. This is so different from how I feel at home, where I'm either yelled at or, worse, ignored for hours.

I just can't help comparing my home life with this one. For years I only knew my own situation and my own relationship with my mother. That was my reality. Getting to occasionally hang out with my girlfriends and their families as a pre-teen provides me with a unique and comparative perspective. The thing I particularly love about being with Robyn at her house is that everyone is in a good mood apart from the occasional arguments she has with her big brother, Eric.

The afternoon playing at Robyn's house is fun and carefree. I like how it feels to be here. No upset. No pressure to do the right thing.

My mom says that Robyn is spoiled. I don't care, because Robyn's house is a friendly place. I love how Mom Colucci talks to me and how she makes me feel. She always asks me how I am and what I like. Then she listens to my answers. I feel like I matter and that what I have to say is important. This is so different from being treated as a snot-brat child who is just supposed to do what she is told to do.

"Do you like chicken?" Mom Colucci asks me.

"Yes, I do," I respond.

"Okay, good," she says. "I'll make chicken for dinner. You're welcome to join us if you're allowed."

Why couldn't I be born into a family like this? Robyn's mother is so hospitable and nurturing.

I wish my mom were like Mom Colucci. For that matter, I wish both my parents were like Robyn's parents.

Why do I have to be in a screwed-up family? I think.

I long for parents I could actually talk to, and for a home where I feel valued. It saddens me that I will soon have to go back to my house. Where life is so different. Where my unpredictable and overly strict mother will dictate my every move. Where her rages of anger result in her whipping me with a wooden spoon until it breaks. I wish I could run away from home and come live with Robyn. But I can only dream about that.

I also often find myself dreaming about moving in with Mom's friend Mrs. Alborn, a beautician who lives with her family just down the street from us. She and Mom go bowling on Mondays when Mom isn't sick. And every couple of months or so, she comes to our house to give us haircuts. She usually sits me in the tall kitchen chair and puts a smock around me before she trims my hair. She's always smiling and always laughing. You can see the little laughter wrinkles around her eyes from all the laughing she does. I've always looked up to her, mostly because she has such a natural way of leaving you feeling happy just from being around her.

By default, I find myself becoming friends with her daughter, Brenda. When I'm at their house, I like spending time talking to Mrs. Alborn. She's always so interested in what I have to say and what I like. She's a good listener. I feel like I can tell her anything and she'll understand. I just love that. For once, I finally feel like I matter.

One Sunday afternoon, I look outside my side bedroom window to see Mrs. Alborn walking down the sidewalk with her hair-cutting supply bag. Mom called her earlier and asked if she would come by to cut my hair. I can see her big beautiful smile as she approaches our house.

When she arrives, Mom calls me downstairs. I come quickly.

"Hi, Mrs. Alborn," I say as I give her a hug and a kiss.

"Hi, sweetie."

She pulls out a chair from the kitchen table and puts it in the center of the kitchen. As she chats with Mom, she taps the back of the chair and I hop on up. She gently drapes the smock around me. I can smell her floral perfume. I notice that her makeup is perfectly applied and that she has braided her beautiful long, dark hair, which goes all the way down to her lower back, and feathered her bangs.

She starts trimming the back of my hair as Mom leaves the room to go to the pantry in the basement.

"How are you, sweetheart?" she asks.

"I'm okay."

"How is everything with Mom?"

"Okay," I respond.

I wonder how much she knows about Mom's illness.

"How are you feeling?"

"Okay," I respond, still hesitant to open up to her.

"I bet it can be hard for you to have a mom who doesn't always feel good."

Her words finally reach me, creeping past my resistance.

"Yes, it's hard. I wish the doctor would get her medicine right. I think if he did, Mom would feel better."

"You know a lot of people care about you, right?"

"I guess so."

"Well, I care about you and so does Brenda. If you ever need us, we're just down the street."

Just then we hear Mom come upstairs from the basement and our conversation ends.

Realizing what life is like outside of my home and what I might have if Mom were well is hard. It saddens me when I think that my home life and my relationship with my mother will never be what I want or what I've hoped it could be. Instead, as painful as it is, I learn how to accept the things I cannot change.

CHAPTER 9

Come to My House

IT'S BEEN MONTHS NOW SINCE I've been hanging out with Robyn. She doesn't know why I never invite her over to our house to play. She just thinks that's weird.

Maybe it would be okay to have her over, I think. *Mom hasn't been too volatile lately.* Then immediately I challenge that notion. *No, don't do it, Michelle. You know what happened last time. You thought she was okay because you wanted her to be okay. But she wasn't. She wasn't nearly as stable as you thought she was.*

There are very few people with whom I share my secret about my mom. I fear they'll judge me and say that I have a crazy mom. So I don't tell too many people and I certainly don't invite people over to my house because of how unpredictable she can be.

Every now and then, a glimmer of hope surfaces when I can see periods of stability with Mom's symptoms. I desperately welcome this normal period because it's such an improvement over her totally debilitative or incredibly manic states. Sometimes, I feel like I actually wish these moments into reality partly because I want so badly for the illness to finally go away forever. I do my best to make the most of those times when she seems to have returned to the mom I remember from so long ago.

Today seems to be one of those days. I'm so happy that Mom seems to be so much better. She's not upset or acting manic. She seems stable.

Good, I think. *I can finally invite Robyn over.*

I've really missed hanging out with my friends, but I would never have invited any of them over last week when Mom was so upset and crying so much. What a relief that the doctor has finally given her the right medication and that she's okay now.

Just before Robyn arrives, Mom's behavior suddenly shifts. She becomes increasingly erratic and begins rushing from the kitchen to the dining room and back and forth very quickly.

Oh, no! I think. *What is she doing?*

How am I going to explain my mother's odd behavior to Robyn?

"What's wrong, Mom?" I ask.

"They are gone. They were all stolen."

"What was stolen?" I ask.

"Someone took all the good stuff when I was in the hospital. What else did they take?"

For some reason she has convinced herself that people came into our house and stole her antique china from our china cabinet when she wasn't here.

Not that again, I think.

She proceeds to examine every piece in the china cabinet.

"Shit!" she exclaims, her energy visibly building as she paces from room to room.

The whites of her eyes expand just as they do every time she gets upset. I can almost hear her thoughts racing.

"The second I turn my back! I knew they had an eye on my good china. I can't trust anyone coming into this house when I'm not home. Where is that little glass? Looks like that's gone, too. I knew they would come and take my things. Now part of my grandmother's antique set is missing. Assholes!"

Oh, my God! Why did you think she was well enough for Robyn to come over! You're an idiot, Michelle. She's going to think you're weird because your mother is totally acting crazy.

Before I know it, the doorbell rings. I let Robyn in and quickly try to lead her away from the dining room, where Mom now has the entire contents of our china cabinet sprawled across the dining room table.

At this point, Mom, still acutely focused on the china cabinet, has become vehemently angry. When she gets like this, she has no filter. She's raw and abrasive, and I fear that Robyn will say the wrong thing.

"Hi, Mrs. Dickinson," Robyn says as we pass the dining room.

"I hope you don't have friends that would steal from you!" Mom responds. "You better keep an eye on those things that you value. People are stealing these days. They stole all my china when I wasn't home, and they will steal yours, too."

Robyn looks at me perplexed, as if waiting for my explanation or translation. I just smile and quickly hustle her upstairs to my bedroom. We get into my room and exhale deeply as I slide down the back of the door, which I've shut tight.

"I'm sorry. My mom hasn't been feeling well. She's been a bit sick lately. I think they gave her the wrong medication."

I don't know what else to say to help Robyn forget about the weird encounter. I quickly change the subject and we begin looking at the supplies I have for us to make pretty long ribbon barrettes.

Amazingly, that visit doesn't go too badly. Not like some others.

A few months earlier I had gotten up the courage to invite over Rebecca from across the street, who was here from out of state visiting her grandparents for the weekend. Usually whenever she came into town I would go over to her grandparents' house to play with her. This time I wanted her to come over to play with me and my Barbies and all my cool accessories. When I opened the door to let her in, Mom totally hit the roof because I hadn't asked her permission.

"Who the hell said you could have anyone over, young lady?" Mom yelled as Rebecca was standing right next to me. "You don't deserve any friends. You deserve nothing."

Rebecca was so freaked out that she ran out of the house and across the street as fast as she could run. She didn't come back over to our house again. And after that incident and the one with Robyn, I didn't invite her or anyone else over again. I had learned my lesson.

CHAPTER 10

Manic High Mom

Here and there I get a reprieve from controlling and abusive Mom. Before falling into a deep depression, she often turns manic, which only happens every once in a while, and never lasts long enough. Suddenly, she's not focused on me or on what I'm doing wrong. Instead she is happy.

I love being with my happy mom. I love days like the one when she takes me to our favorite craft store, The Crafty Kitchen. Just walking into that store is a dream come true for me. The smell of cinnamon sticks and the hand-dipped candles literally awakens my senses. Colorful and bright, this massively oversized craft warehouse is lined with rows and rows of an endlessly inviting assortment of materials that invigorate me with pure possibility of what I will create. Mom grabs a shopping cart and starts to stroll down each of the long, narrow, craft-filled aisles. This trip is going to be even better than I thought. I just love looking at all of the craft supplies. There are so many different and new creative craft ideas!

What will we buy today? I ask myself.

The ideas are endless. There is so much that we can create with these supplies. The store has so many craft ideas on display that it's going to be hard to choose.

As we turn the corner of one aisle to head down the next, all I can see is a beautiful wall of all different-colored silk flowers. Across from the flowers are rows and rows of beautiful satin ribbons in every color of the rainbow. Toward the end of the next aisle, an entire section dedicated to chocolate candy making draws my eye. Stacks of cellophane-filled bags of white, milk and dark chocolate wafers line the shelving. The display of chocolate candy molds is taller than I am.

"Mom, can we get these lollipop-shaped molds so that I can make chocolate lollipops? Please, please, please!" I ask.

"Sure!" she says without hesitation.

This is so great, I think as I place the molds, lollipop sticks and the bags of milk chocolate wafers into our shopping cart.

Finally, we reach the end of the last aisle in the store, the needlepoint section. The right side of the display is filled with clear mesh canvas shapes and sizes along with an assortment of patterns. The top shelf showcases examples of all the crafts that you can make using plastic mesh canvas, with everything from ornaments to tissue box covers made in yarn-covered plastic mesh. The back wall of the store is lined with cubbies stuffed with different textured yarns in any color imaginable.

Lately, Mom has had a real affinity for making canvas projects. Mom always has her hands in a variety of craft projects. When she finds something she enjoys, she dives right in! Last year just before Christmas, she made a beautiful train set with an accompanying village made out of this plastic mesh needlepoint. The village consisted of multicolored tall and short buildings. The small train set included several different colored cars, including a small coal car that would sit just behind the engine. I loved that Mom put black jellybeans in the coal car representing coal. Not only was that creative, when she wasn't looking I could steal a jellybean. Once the entire set was assembled, it was beautiful. You would never know that the display was made of plastic canvas.

I can only imagine what Mom's artistic mind is thinking about making today! Declaring that we'll be making a full set of Christmas tree ornaments, she collects all the supplies we need. After filling the cart with plastic mesh sheets, patterns and needles, she begins tossing in a variety of different-colored yarns.

As we walk toward the cash register, Mom grabs items that we don't even need for our needlepoint project. Bags of glue sticks, bunches of silk flowers and rolls of macramé sit on top of the shopping cart that's piled high. There is just no way that we will be able to make all of these crafts, especially since Mom is not consistent. She generally starts projects and then loses interest. Even now, all our closets are stuffed with materials for all kinds of crafts she's abandoned along the way.

Behind the cash register I can see small buckets of handmade candy sticks in all different flavors and colors.

"Mom, can I have a cherry candy stick?"

Yay! I say to myself when she agrees.

As we hand the items to the cashier, we quickly run out of counter space. When everything is rung up and placed in plastic bags, the cash register reads $300. Mom pulls out the $300 in cash from the white bank envelope in her purse without flinching.

Wow, that's a lot of money, I say to myself. *Mom is rich today*.

After our shopping spree in the craft store, we get in the car. Mom turns to me.

"Do you want to go out to lunch today?"

"Yes!" I answer without a second's hesitation. "Where are we going?"

"Let's go to Friendly's."

The magic that is today continues. Mom laughs the entire time we are together. She's clearly feeling wonderful today. After the sad, dark days of her depression this is paradise, especially since I can do no wrong. She suddenly seems to love everything about me. She seems high on life, too. For just a short snapshot in time, I feel like I have a normal mom in my life. In the back of my mind, I know that this will not last, so I drink in how loving, caring and nurturing she is toward me.

After our lunch, we return home. Piles of multicolored yarn fill one end of our dining room table. Adjacent to the yarn lie packets of small silver needles and needlepoint instruction patterns. I reach for the large stack of clear mesh plastic canvas sheets and one of the two sets of Mom's best craft scissors in front of me, and Mom and I laugh as we begin cutting out different shapes and patterns in the clear plastic sheets on the table. The silliest things seem so funny.

Before long, my ribs ache from all of the giggling. It's so much fun being with Mom when she is this happy. This is the mom that I love the most. When she is happy and carefree, she's my favorite person in the entire world. This is my magical mom.

Thank God, I say to myself. *It's been a while since I've had my real mom back.*

The late-afternoon sunlight spills into the dining room just above the chestnut-stained window shutters. Teddy is bathing in the sun on the floor in the one sunspot that he can find near us on the dining room floor. In the kitchen, Mom's radio plays energizing oldies music while the salty smell of Mom's ham and split pea soup fills the entire downstairs. The gold chandelier hanging above the dining room table illuminates our colorful variety of craft supplies.

This is the best day ever! I say to myself, savoring how awesome it feels to be at home with my mom right now. *I don't want this day to end.* I wish Mom could always be this happy.

As we sit at the dining room table making our ornaments together, Mom feels the impulse to put on her favorite record, *Pac-Man Fever.* I hear the click of the record player dropping the album and the music begins to play. She turns up the volume so loud that the room vibrates. Then she starts singing and dancing around the living room, her face illuminated with joy. She's so carefree. Her smile is big, and her mood is euphoric. Someone on the outside looking in might perceive this as crazy. Not me. I'm elated and hugely relieved to finally witness her happy again. This moment is perfect and I do not want anything to interrupt it, even though I know there will be a price to pay for today's exorbitant spending.

A few weeks later, I see Dad hunched over a sea of papers on the dining table upon which Mom and I so happily made our needlepoint crafts. His face is red and his body language tense as he sorts through the papers. He shakes his head.

"Seriously, you spent that kind of money?" he yells at Mom. "How are we going to pay our bills this month?"

Dad is angry. Really angry. I can tell from Mom's sunken posture that she's equally upset. I try to stay out of the way so that they don't take their anger out on me.

Time with my happy and joyful mom is never long enough. I want that mom always. I wish she realized that her meds help her feel so good. Instead, every time she gets manic she decides she doesn't need them. Which inevitably leads to a downward spiral.

Sometimes, she nosedives even if she keeps taking them, because they just stop working. It's always hard to figure out if we're dealing with noncompliance or ineffectiveness when she becomes unwell. Either way, most of the time, just like today, I'm saddled with a sick and sad mom. And it sucks! I hate being stuck as Mom's caretaker and unable to go to school. None of my friends have to do this. Why do I?

I fantasize about my happy mom. I want that mom back. I want the caring and supportive mom who shows up every now and then. Happy mom is easy and fun to be with. I want that mom back. I don't want this mom.

"It's not fair!" I want to scream, but it's like opening my mouth and not having a voice, so nothing comes out.

As always, Mom tanks after her fabulous manic period. As her crying intensifies over the following days, I know there's nothing I can do to console her.

Later that day, Dad comes home from work a little early so that he can call the doctor. I overhear him on the phone.

"She's sad and crying, and she says she has no energy," Dad says to the doctor. "She says she doesn't like how the medication makes her feel, so she stopped taking the pills."

Dad asks the doctor to change Mom's medications. A short while later the drug store delivers us her new prescription. Because of the medication change, over the next few days Mom becomes a little more stable. The crying subsides. At least she's stable enough for me to go back to school. I've been home for four days in a row, and I know I'm going to have a lot of work to make up.

Just because she seems a little more stable doesn't mean that everything is going to be perfect when I get home from school. I know that I can anticipate a bumpy road ahead. The new medications always work initially. But that never lasts long.

As I sit in algebra class the next day, I gaze outside the window and find myself worrying about Mom.

Concentrate, Michelle! Pay attention! I think to myself. *You can't fail algebra again!*

My admonitions don't work.

I wonder if she's okay. I hope she didn't have Dad paged again at work.

Now I'm getting myself all worked up.

It's okay, I say to myself, trying to calm myself. *Just a few more classes and I can get home to check on her.*

I know that if I can just make her laugh and get her to focus on something, she will come out of her sadness. I know I can make a difference and when I do Dad will be so pleased and I will get my mom back.

I really need to get home today. I can just feel it. I need to know how she is. I rush right home after school through the cold rain and arrive home soaked.

Plumes of white cigarette smoke fill our dimly lit living room, which feels damp and dirty and smells of smoke and burned coffee. Mom sits in her chair, still in her red satin pajamas, her hair unbrushed. Her large ceramic ashtray overflows with ashes, extinguished cigarette butts, empty candy wrappers and yet another lit cigarette. It hits me that she hasn't showered for days now. She doesn't appear to care about how she looks. Why didn't I notice this sooner? Why didn't I pay more attention to this? That's a major sign that I totally missed.

As she crochets, tears stream down her flushed face with its large dark bags under her eyes. I fill up with a sick, familiar feeling of deep sadness. Mom is not okay. She is in that dark place of total despair once again. As usual, I had hoped we would not get to this point.

In the kitchen, piled-up dirty dishes and soiled pots from the previous four days have now filled up both sides of the sink. Plates with dried-on food sit stacked up on the countertop because there is no more space in the sink. The rest of the kitchen counter and stovetop is filthy with food, crumbs and dried-up sauces and is stained with cup rings from where beverages have overflowed. It looks like I'm going to have to dig us out from under this mess again or we won't be able to prepare dinner.

I sit down on the ottoman at her feet and try talking to her.

"Mom, what is wrong?" I ask.

She just looks at me and shakes her head. "Nothing."

She begins to cry again. She won't even try to articulate an answer to me. She just continues to cry, and as usual I have no idea why.

Something must be wrong, because my mind can't comprehend how someone could cry for so long for no reason. I try talking to her while I'm rubbing her leg. I begin to tell her about my day to try to distract her.

"I got a B on my social studies test and in Spanish class I mixed up the word *door* with *mouth*. So when the teacher asked me in Spanish to close the door, I closed my mouth instead. I made the entire class laugh. It was so funny."

She just looks at me with tears in her eyes, not reacting to my story.

When my attempts at trying to make her laugh don't work, I just hug her tightly, and tell her that I love her and it will all be okay. Why can't my loving her so much just fix everything and make her feel better? I feel like my hands are tied. I need to get better at this, so I can reach her and help pull her out of this sadness.

What's wrong with me? I think.

Once again, I absorb her feelings of hopelessness and despair. There is nothing that I can do right now to help stop her pain or my own. But perhaps I can at least stem the sobbing.

"You know that Dad will be coming home soon. You don't want to be upset when he comes home from work."

She stops sobbing for a brief moment. She knows that when Dad comes home, he's going to yell at her to "snap out of it."

That works sometimes. Dad's presence can force some normalcy in our house. Compelled to play the role of mom and wife regardless of her sadness, she'll make us dinner and some form of structure will return.

She's too far gone this time. Dad yelling at her just propels her deeper into her sadness and crying. Sobbing hysterically, Mom starts to spiral out of control.

"Mom, it's okay!"

I grab her and hug her, and begin to cry myself.

"Mom, I love you. Please stop crying," I whisper to her.

I can't do anything to make it better.

Feeling helpless, I escape to my bedroom. From the upstairs hallway, I look back down through the banister spindles and see her just sitting there in her chair weeping. I can't even watch.

How come Dad isn't doing anything to help her? I ask myself.

We're in trouble now. She's going to have to go to the hospital again.

I should have known this was coming and done something. I should have been able to stop it before it got this far. I should have been able to distract her and make her laugh. This is all my fault.

CHAPTER 11

Hospital Mom

WHEN THE FULL-BLOWN EPISODES HIT, Mom is usually hospitalized for several weeks. Reluctantly, Dad drives her to Carrier Clinic to have her admitted. He never takes me with him when he does this. He has my grandma come and take care of me so that I'm not alone.

At a certain moment after my dad takes her away, a deep sense of calmness and relief pervades our house, a tranquility that I can still feel to this day. Suddenly the sadness and suffering are over. Watching Mom's painful tears and nervous shaking, along with the related sense of chaos, is behind us for now.

They say that treatment for bipolarity provides patients with a road map to be able to ride the ups and downs of life and tame the emotions. This isn't always the case. When Mom is initially admitted to the hospital in a severe state, she often receives electroconvulsive therapy (ECT), a dreadful treatment known as the therapy that curbs the wildness of bipolarity. ECT is described as a tool that pulls the severely depressed out of the darkness. It's argued that the treatment isn't as bad as people make it out to be, but I can't see how that can be true. With ECT, they literally place electrodes on your head and shoot an electric current into your brain, causing all of your nerves to react and your body to convulse. To have to willingly undergo that treatment must be horrifying for Mom. Even worse, I'm sure that my father is the one who has to authorize the treatment. That makes my heart sink because I'm sure that he knows how much she dreads that treatment.

After a few weeks of Mom being in the hospital, we're finally able to see her. Every few nights during the week, we load up in the red Mercury Marquis after dinner and make the forty-five-minute drive to Carrier Clinic so that we can spend some time with her.

The hospital smells funny and seems bare and sterile.

I hate being here, I think to myself. *None of my friends have to visit their moms in the hospital. Why should I?*

Dad speaks to the woman at the front desk. Soon an orderly appears and escorts us down the long white sterile hallway to Mom's room. He is talking to Dad, but I can't hear what he is saying because he's whispering.

Mom is medicated and is in somewhat of a zombie state. That doesn't matter to me. I may hate having to visit her in this hospital, but I'm thrilled to see her. Regardless of how dysfunctional it is at home with her controlling, abusive and often needy states, she's still my mother and I miss her.

As we walk down the hall, I fantasize that her hospital treatment has fixed her. Part of me clings to the illusion that this time when she comes home she'll be that loving and caring mother I once had so long ago. In my heart I know better. We have gone through this before.

Mom sits on the corner of her bed in her small hospital room that contains only a bed and a small dresser. I can tell that she has showered, and her hair is combed. She is wearing clean slacks and a sweater. She gives me a hug but seems distant because of all of the treatment and medication that she is on. My once tough-as-nails mother who is so often a force to be reckoned with has lost all of her power. It's hard for me to see her there so sick.

"Look," she says, removing a small pink, blue and purple triangular yarn ornament hanging from the lamp switch on her dresser. "I made this in an art class yesterday. It's called *God's Eye.*"

I smile. "It's beautiful, Mom."

Whatever craft Mom makes always comes out pretty, even when she's in this condition, because she is so naturally talented.

Dad hugs Mom and she starts to cry. They're tears of happiness this time because she's so happy we've come to visit. As they embrace, I look around at her barren hospital room. It's so strange for me to realize that she lives there now.

Eventually we have to say goodbye and leave for home without her. That's the hardest part. She's so far away from us in the hospital. It makes me feel so sad and alone. I love my dad, but he won't tuck me in or hug me like Mom does when she feels good.

I'm sure being left behind is equally as hard, if not worse, for Mom. I can't imagine having to deal with being pulled from the game of life, however temporarily, unable to be a wife and a mother to your own family.

Upon our return, the house is quiet, peaceful. I hang up my coat and head upstairs to put on my pajamas. Dad makes us each a bowl of heavenly hash ice cream with hot fudge and whipped cream. We sit down and watch *T.J. Hooker* on TV together. Dad and I love watching this show.

I get to sit in Mom's recliner. I always like sitting here because it's one of the most comfortable chairs in the house, but tonight it feels weird. The chair smells like her perfume. I try to look past her ashtray and crochet hooks on the end table as I eat my ice cream and then lie back to watch our program.

The show ends, and without Dad telling me, like a well-trained little soldier, I head to the bathroom to brush my teeth. I know it's time for bed.

What a great evening, I think as I close my eyes. After all the drama during Mom's rapid decline and after all the tears mixed with tension and being on edge, I can start to feel my body slowly unwind and relax. I'm finally able to let my guard down. Nobody will abruptly throw open my bedroom door and relentlessly scream at me. I won't have to caretake tonight, tomorrow night or the night after. I'm temporarily free from that horrible sickness that has consumed us and made our lives so difficult.

Almost immediately, those positive thoughts and feelings are abruptly shortened by a strong sense of guilt.

What about Mom? What about the cold and sterile hospital room she's stuck in? She doesn't belong in a place like that. She should be home with us.

I try to stop myself from thinking about how she must feel, but I can't. Tears stream down my face.

Why is there always something wrong? I ask myself as I fall asleep.

Weeks go by and Mom is finally released from the hospital. I'm so excited that she's finally coming home to us. I've begun to realize that the only real reason Mom gets so mean is because she's so sick. And that after she comes home from the hospital and her shock therapy, she's always incredibly peaceful. For a little while, she's the mom I remember. My real mom. I treasure this brief window of time more than anything.

I see the car pull up. Mom is finally back where she belongs!

She walks slowly and calmly through the doorway and into the house. Dad holds her hand as he guides her up the stairs from the back door. I run to her and throw my arms around her waist.

"Mommy, Mommy, you're home!" I exclaim.

She wraps her arms around me. I revel in the warmth of her hug. She kisses my head before sitting down at the kitchen table. For a moment, I'm able to temporarily forget about how hard life can be with her. I want to believe all that will never happen again.

That's all behind us now, I conclude, eager yet again to dwell in the fantasy of Mom being well forever despite knowing deep down that this won't be the reality.

Dad pours Mom a glass of water, as Teddy cries with excitement and jumps up and down on her legs. She leans down and picks him up. When he kisses her entire face, she laughs in a joyful, lighthearted way.

"Hi, baby," she says to Teddy.

Even her face, with its skin so smooth it seems to be made of cream, seems relaxed. There is no trace of the sadness or angst that I'm so used to seeing. Her kind smile reflects her renewed lightness along with a gentle softness that I want to capture forever.

That first evening back, she almost acts like a guest in her own house, a house where she usually has full and complete command. As Dad starts a pot of coffee, she sits quiet and reserved at the kitchen table, gazing outside at the yard. Soon the smell of the brewing coffee fills the kitchen. Our house is finally a home again.

I love that this version of Mom is so entirely different from the person she has become. Not only are the extreme sadness and the intense nervousness gone, she's loving toward me. I gulp it down like a cold drink of water I have been thirsting for. When I share my school day experiences with her, she listens attentively, which she never does normally. It feels like everything is right again, and I never want this feeling to end. Life has returned to the normal that I always dream about and that disappeared so many years ago.

Maybe this is it, I think. *Maybe Mom has finally gotten the correct treatment.*

I convince myself that this mom will stay—the mom I always knew was in there and who really loves me. This time will finally be different. This time will be forever.

I'll be a good girl, I promise myself. *This time I'm not going to misbehave so that Mom has to get upset and yell at me.*

I know that I can cause her to have a nervous breakdown when I misbehave. I remember the last time I was bad.

"Dad, why is Mom so upset again? Didn't they adjust her medication?"

"Well, you don't help, Michelle. You don't listen to your mother. That's why she has to yell at you and it gets her nervous and upset. Why don't you just behave?"

"I didn't mean to spill the water on the floor, Dad."

"Well, just watch what you're doing and behave! Period. Then she won't get so upset," he says forcefully to me.

The thought of me causing my mom to get sick makes me cry.

How could I be so stupid? Everything would be fine if it weren't for me.

I have to be on my best behavior from now on so that she doesn't get nervous and upset again. If she does, she'll get sick and it will be my fault.

Just be good, Michelle, I say to myself again and again. *Just behave.*

As the weeks roll by, Mom begins participating in parenting me again. Instead of being aggressive and mean like she once was, she continues to be nurturing and loving. Part of me feels like this is her way of apologizing for being so cruel without actually saying the words. Then the side effects of her treatment start to show up.

I've read that often manic depression patients are actually more afraid of the medication and treatment than they are of their own illness. They know all too well about the side effects, which with ECT include memory loss. And, although I'm my mom's world during the weeks following shock therapy and her return home, she turns increasingly unfamiliar and distant, often forgetting details from past events.

"Mom, I did it!" I exclaim to her as I come bouncing into the house.

"Did what?" she says to me.

"I climbed the big rope to the very top in gym class today!"

"Good for you," she responds. "I'm sure that you did it easily."

What did she just say?

"Mom, you remember what happened the last time I tried to climb the rope, right?"

"No."

"How can you have forgotten that, Mom? Don't you remember how I slid down the rope and got rope burns all across my hands and legs? It was so horrible."

"When did that happen?"

"Last year."

I can't believe that she doesn't remember this. The school called her, and she had to come pick me up and take me to see Dr. Mayer and get my hands and legs treated. How could she not remember?

I realize that the ECT treatment helps make her emotionally stronger. However, once those idyllic few weeks following her return to the hospital pass, it also seems to weaken our mother–daughter relationship, which is already strained. And, it freaks me out when I realize that her memory loss extends from significant experiences to something as simple as driving us to a familiar store.

Mom and I hop in the car and head to a specialty card store called Irma's Bag in nearby Fanwood, a town just five miles from our house. She backs out of our driveway and pulls the gearshift on the steering column to put the car into drive. Suddenly she brakes. As soon as the car comes to a stop, she looks at me. I can tell her mind is starting to race.

"I can go this way or the other way," she says. "Maybe we should go the other way. Or, I can go that back way, too. I wonder which way we should go."

As we proceed down our street to the corner, she begins making a right-hand turn onto the busy tree-lined main road, a road that many people get pulled over on by the police because of speeding. Midway into the turn she changes her mind and suddenly turns left. Cars honk as she cuts in front of them, and Mom begins to shake. This repeats over and over the entire fifteen-minute trip to the store. She's forgetful and unable to focus on which way she wants to go. She's like a scurrying mouse just zipping around. Her inability to focus on anything for more than thirty seconds is fine when she's rushing around from cabinet to cabinet at home, but it becomes incredibly frightening when we're in the car together and trying to get someplace.

I know that Mom's illness and hospitalizations take a toll on my dad, too. It's hard to watch him try to manage her. Eventually, with enough time, things start to return to normal.

About eight weeks after Mom's return from the hospital, Dad starts feeling a bit more confident that Mom has stabilized. I can tell because he's invited company over for dinner this evening. In just a short time Dad's friend from work is coming over with his wife.

Dad is helping Mom prepare dinner in the kitchen, when suddenly she begins to cry.

"Why are you crying?" Dad asks in an irritated tone.

"I don't know," Mom replies as she whimpers.

"How can you be crying if you don't know why you're crying?"

"I don't know."

At this, she begins to cry even harder.

"Stop it," Dad demands. "Stop crying!"

"I can't. I'm sorry, but I can't!"

"Stop crying and snap out of it already," Dad says with a raised voice. "Our company is going to be here soon. Just snap out of it!"

His words have no effect.

"If you don't snap out of it soon, we are going to have to go back to the hospital again," he threatens. "Just calm yourself!"

Mom continues to cry. She sits down at the kitchen table, unable to cook. Dad just doesn't understand. No matter what he says to her, she can't control her emotions like a switch.

Dad knows too little about Mom's illness, and his lack of understanding makes him fear it all the more. To be honest, neither he nor I truly understand what she's going through or how she feels being bipolar. All we can do is just watch from the sidelines, and sometimes even that is too hard. In this painful process, we find ourselves getting battered and bruised just observing the struggle.

PART 2
The Toll

CHAPTER 12

Escaping Home Life

As tough as growing up with a mentally ill mother was as a youngster, it only gets harder once I begin to pursue my independence and search for my identity. As a teenager, I cling to my girlfriends and to a daily routine that has me in school, far away from my confusing and trying home environment.

It's Monday morning and I'm in my bedroom getting dressed for school. I need to leave on time today so that I'm not late to meet my best friend, Katie, with whom I walk to school every day. I feel like Katie is my twin sister. We've been best friends for a long time, and I adore her. She knows what it's like at home for me with my mom. She understands. I can trust her and share with her my feelings about my mom. She's a safe haven for me.

I put on my favorite clothes, grab my lunch bag and head out for my walk down to Dorian Road, where she lives. I reach her house and knock on the front door. Her mom greets me at the door.

"Hi, Michelle," she says. "How are you today?"

"Hi, Mrs. Mondelli. I'm good."

"How is Mom doing, sweetie?"

I find myself always having to give an update on my mom's condition, which is the last thing I want to do since it forces me to reflect on exactly how she was when I left her.

"She's doing okay," I reply.

"Good," she says. "I'm happy to hear that. Katie is upstairs just finishing getting dressed. She'll be right down."

I adore Katie's parents. Her mom and dad are so friendly and easygoing. Their home feels different from mine, full of warmth and love. Even Katie's big sister, Mary Beth, is sweet to me. Mary Beth, who's in high school now, always looks so pretty the way she dresses and curls her hair. I hope I'll be that pretty when I grow up. Every morning I watch her and Katie's mom put on their makeup in front of the old wooden mirror that sits above the vanity just inside their front door. The top drawer is filled with makeup brushes, eye makeup, all different kinds of blush and a variety of lipsticks. It's a young girl's dream come true!

Katie comes downstairs and heads to the vanity to apply her makeup.

"Can I use some makeup, too?" I ask. My mom doesn't let me wear any makeup, so this would be a real treat.

"Sure," Katie replies. I watch Katie put on her eye shadow and liner, and copy just how she does it. Then we apply some blush to our cheeks.

It's springtime in Westfield, so it's mild outside. Today we're both wearing matching miniskirts. I love it when we dress alike because you can tell that we're best friends. We have also become class flirts with the boys at school, and the boys also like it when we wear miniskirts.

We begin our walk to school together, chatting the entire way. For a short period of time, I'm happy. I have temporarily paused all my worries about what's going on at home with my mom.

All that changes once summer hits. With school out, I no longer have a daily place to escape to. I can't even spend time with Katie or my other friends. During the summer months, my family packs up the car and we head to our beach house on the lagoon in Mystic Island. It will be months until I get to see my buddies again. And I don't have many friends down the shore, which leaves me feeling isolated and alone.

I decide to walk to the Italian restaurant on the marina down the road and apply for a waitress job to help pass the time. The restaurant has a casual pizzeria area as well as a dining room overlooking the water that serves full Italian dinners. The waitresses carry giant trays on their shoulders, which initially intimidates me. I'm used to carrying plates of food, but not such oversized trays. Regardless, I get the job and quickly find that I'm working every weekend and several evenings during the week. I don't mind. The staff and the customers are all very kind to me, and the long hours provide me with an escape from the emotional stress at home.

I quickly learn that I can make a lot of money in tips by working hard, being nice to customers and providing them with good service. So I immerse myself in my work, finding solace in this friendly and predictable environment. I'm able to save up a lot of money while still having enough to splurge some on pretty-smelling beauty products. When not at work, I spend my time on the back deck tanning, listening to my boom box and trying to stay out of my mom's way.

When I get older, I start to feel a little less trapped once I get my driver's license. I look for any excuse to go out. I hop into my tan Subaru hatchback and drive anyplace I can think of so that I don't have to be home in that toxic, heavy environment. I know the roads around me. I have been paying attention since I was little, just waiting for this moment to come.

The first time I can finally drive myself, I decide to head up to the Watchung Mountains, a wonderful wooded area on the reservation just a short drive from my house.

Maybe I'll even keep going when I reach the mountains, I think.

The winding road has a way of showcasing the magnitude of trees and diversity of the hills. I feel so small compared with the wall of tall trees that seems to go on forever. With my windows rolled down, the breeze filled with the scent of pine and dry leaves blows through the car.

Invigorated by the sense of freedom that consumes me, I drive faster. For a short moment in time, I have nobody hovering over me and telling me what to do. It's intoxicating. I don't care about the time. I don't care about the rules or my curfew. I just want to submerge myself in the feeling of not being trapped in our boring, painful home.

As I drive around the winding roads of the reservation listening to Janet Jackson, I fantasize about never having to go home again and what that would be like. I have this car that can take me anywhere I want now. I think of where I could drive to that would take me far away from the confines of my difficult home life. I allow time to drift by as I drive the open roads of the forest.

By the time I return home, my curfew has long passed. I'm quickly grounded for not following the rules. Again. Being grounded means I'm forced to stay in my home environment, and I hate it. There is no aliveness or autonomy. I feel like a noose has been hung around my neck. With my movements restricted, I feel totally controlled. I have come to despise that the most.

CHAPTER 13

Not Comfortable in My Own Skin

IT'S THAT TIME OF THE DAY. School is back in session, second period is about to end, and I dread going to third period. I don't want to go to my gym class, which I actually really enjoy. However, to get into class I first have to change into my gym clothes in the locker room, which I absolutely hate. I don't like how my body looks and I don't want anyone to see me naked, even for a short moment. I feel especially chubby today, so the stakes are even higher than usual.

I only have five minutes to get changed and get out onto the gym floor or I'll get in trouble. I head into the locker room and deploy the strategy I've developed for undressing in the locker room. First, I face my locker. Holding my gym T-shirt between my legs, I pull my blouse over my head, grab my T-shirt and pull it back over my head, covering myself as quickly as possible. Then I turn around with my back to my locker and bend over at the waist to pull off my pants. Grabbing my sweatpants as fast as I can, I quickly step into them and yank them up. The entire process takes less than ten seconds.

A girl in my class looks over at me.

"Why do you get dressed so weird?"

I say nothing. I don't even know how to respond. Then it comes to me and I pull the answer out of thin air.

"I like getting dressed quickly so that I can go wash my face."

I don't want the other girls in our locker space to think I'm weird.

Thankfully the locker room isn't too busy today, so I don't have too many girls to avoid. The other day, it was different. The locker room was totally packed, and my locker area was filled with girls changing. I was so freaked out that I took my clothes to the bathroom stalls that day, which caused me to get onto the gym floor late.

I really wish that undressing weren't so hard for me. I wish that I could just forget what I saw late that one afternoon. I mean, I didn't ask to see it. I was being a good kid, sitting on my bed in my bedroom doing my homework when it happened.

Mom has just finished showering. She begins singing and dancing in the hallway.

Hmmm, that's good. I guess the shower put her in a good mood.

As she gets louder, I peek out of the corner of the bedroom doorway to see what's up. What a stupid mistake! She's completely naked, running up and down the hallway dancing and singing. As if that isn't bad enough, she catches me peeking out of the doorway, which seems to encourage her even more.

Mom's sickness causes her weight to fluctuate. She has recently lost a good bit of weight, so the excess skin, which is that much more pronounced, vibrates as she jiggles her arms and legs. She starts singing even louder.

I'm mortified. How could she run around like this without any concern? I try to ignore her, but she dances her way into my room.

"This is it, Michelle," she yells. "This is the female body and what you have to look forward to!"

Ugh, I don't want to look like that, I think.

I'm terrified. When I look at her naked body, all I can see is crazy. It's hard to comprehend how she feels no embarrassment, shame or concern for how she looks.

The sight of her just makes me want to cover myself up. As soon as she leaves my room, I grab a blanket and wrap it around me. No wonder I'm so self-conscious, private and overly worried about anyone seeing me undress.

CHAPTER 14

My Pity Party

THE UNCOMFORTABLE FEELING I experience in my own body is mirrored by how awkward I feel in any kind of social situation. It's Saturday night. Alone in my bedroom, I lie on my red floral bedspread just staring up at my small TV set situated on the corner of my tall dresser. As the breeze blows into my room from the two front windows, the matching red drapes dance in the wind. Normally that would make me happy. Not tonight. I know that my friends are all at a house party on the other side of town right now. I was at Katie's house until late last night, so Mom says I can't go out again tonight. House rules dictate that I can only go out one night a weekend.

While part of me is upset about not being able to hang out with them, another part is relieved. I'm not good at being in large group situations like a house party. I like hanging out one-on-one more. That way I don't experience the horror of trying to fit in like that time at John's Bar Mitzvah. I relive that memory often.

There I am at the reception hall for the celebration party after temple that's packed with some two hundred kids. Everyone is laughing and having a good time. Everyone but me, that is. As my anxiety starts to mount, I find a small table in the corner of the reception hall far away from the dance floor. It will be hours before my mom comes to pick me up. I don't know how I'm going to last.

Jenny comes over. "Why are you sitting over here all alone, Michelle?" she asks me.

"Oh, I'm just not feeling well," I reply.

I'm totally lying. I'm just incredibly uncomfortable being in this situation. Many of the kids are classmates, with the addition of a number of others I don't know. Either way, I don't know how to break into the small groups of kids gathering around the perimeter of the dance floor. The thought of interacting with them completely terrifies me.

I hate this. I just want to be home right now, alone in my predictable and familiar house. Jenny leaves and I sit there in the corner, hoping that nobody else sees me or notices that I'm not near the dance floor. I don't know why I can't just fit in and have fun at these kinds of events.

I have gotten used to being alone at home. I even like it sometimes. Mom has set the example and I'm just following it. But that makes it hard for me when I'm in a crowd. Maybe I needed a teacher to show me how to handle these social situations. Or, maybe I just don't know how to be friends. Mom barely has any friends—one or two at the most who rarely come around.

Although I sometimes thirst for social connection, I struggle with the same challenges each day in high school when I see my hundreds of classmates. This usually happens after I've spent weeks being home caring for my mom. As much as I get excited about returning to school and want to hang out with my classmates and the few friends I've managed to make, I just don't know how to do that in a natural way. Instead I rely on luring them to interact with me any way I can.

The easiest way to do this is to share gossip. If I can offer them some juicy tidbit, I can momentarily win their attention and gain their respect. So, there I am sitting in my Spanish class just before the bell rings. The teacher has not yet arrived. I lean over the side of my desk toward the kids sitting around me.

"Hey, did you guys hear about Timmy?" I ask.

Suddenly all eyes are on me. Yes! Victory!

"Mr. Jones smacked Timmy during math class. He finally got tired of him mouthing off! Then, Timmy's father came to the school, found Mr. Jones and punched *him* in the face! Can you believe that? Now Timmy's been expelled and Mr. Jones removed from the classroom."

Shock at my news gives way to laughter. For a brief moment, the kids look at me with admiration, impressed at my inside gossip track. In that moment, I feel liked and acknowledged, even though I know it's just temporary.

What is wrong with me? Why can't I connect with my classmates and friends easily like everyone else? Why am I so awkward and different? Why am I so fearful of people's judgment and so in need of their acceptance? Ugh. Life is just easier when I'm home, isolated with Mom. Most of the time, she sleeps the days away and I get to be by myself.

After all the time alone, I've learned how to entertain myself. I ride my bike or play alone for hours. What started as a requirement in our house has become my safe space. Besides, I have come to realize that to most kids I'm invisible, just like I am at home.

CHAPTER 15

Unseen

I WAS OUT ALL LAST WEEK AGAIN, taking care of Mom. For once, I was able to help her. She seems much more stable because I stayed with her last week. But I'm sure looking forward to returning to school and seeing my friends today. I wonder if they missed me, or if they wondered where I've been. I really miss them. As much as I like hanging out by myself, it's been a bit lonely at home all alone with Mom for this long.

Lunchtime finally comes, and I meet up with my friends as usual in the cafeteria. I open the door to the school cafeteria. The space is large and filled with tables and kids talking and laughing as they linger from last period. I can smell the french fries cooking, and I see a small line at the booth in the corner of the cafeteria where they make the best milkshakes with rainbow sprinkles.

I reach the picnic-style table where I usually eat my lunch, drop my books and head to the food line.

The line isn't too bad today, I think as I grab my tray.

I order my usual lunch—a tuna fish sandwich and french fries—grateful as always that I'm not eating those soggy tomato sandwiches Mom keeps serving. I can't wait to talk to everyone. I make my way back to the lunch table, anticipating how happy they'll be to see me and the questions they'll ask about where I was all last week.

Prepared for all the attention I think I'm about to receive, I start to sit down.

"Hi, guys!" I say enthusiastically.

No one even looks up at me. They certainly don't say anything.

I plunk my tray down, but they keep right on talking about an incident that happened during lunch last week when I was home with my mom. Apparently, the incident involved a few of the ninth-graders. I don't know the full story, and nobody even bothers to fill me in.

"Hey, what happened?" I ask. "What was that about?"

They just keep talking. I turn quiet and the conversation continues without me. It's like I'm not even there.

Out of sheer frustration, I attempt to break into the conversation. They just talk right over me. It's like what I have to say or add is just not important. I feel dismissed and muted. Just when I need their support the most, my voice isn't even being heard.

I don't want to be here, I think. *I thought that these were my friends and that they cared about me. I don't matter to them at all. Why didn't I just stay home today?*

CHAPTER 16

Learning to Accept My
Home Life and Situation

*O*h, my gosh, I'm such a moron. How could I have been so stupid?

I toggle among shame, anger and confusion, trying to make sense of it all.

How is what I said really so bad? I don't understand. Patty did the same thing just last week. What's the big deal?

No matter how many times I try to replay and change things in my head, everything still happens the same exact way. If there were any way to take back the actions of the day, I would in a heartbeat. An emptiness in the pit of my stomach just lingers as the tears spill down my cheeks.

The morning started out fine. Everything was great when I got to school.

"Hey, Kimberly, how are you today?" I ask on my way to first period.

I know that I shouldn't tell her what Tina told me yesterday. But if I do, I know I'll get her attention.

"Did you hear who Tina likes?" I ask.

"No!" she responds, clearly intrigued.

"She likes Brian now! Can you believe it?"

"What? How do you know that?"

"Tina told me and told me not to tell anyone. But I wanted to tell you."

I just want to fit in and be liked by my girlfriends. For some reason, people just seem to share things with me. And my friends like the fact that I often have an inside scoop. Leveraging this has always worked well for me in the past. The last time I shared a secret with them, they loved me for it. But not this time!

Before I know it, I find myself caught up in a gossip triangle. It turns out that Kimberly already knows whom Tina liked. To make matters worse, Kimberly goes back and tells Tina that I told her secret. And now, it's all about how Michelle is a gossip and can't keep a secret. Everyone has sided with Kimberly and Tina instead of me, and now they don't want to be friends anymore. Stupid, stupid me!

How did this happen? My girlfriends are everything to me. I can't imagine not having them anymore. Imagining a life without girlfriends is terrifying. All I did was share one small thing and now I have lost all my friends. I don't know what to do now. I have totally screwed up. I want more than anything to just go home and cry and talk to my mom about what happened.

In that moment I stop myself.

That's never going to be possible, Michelle, I say to myself. *Don't even think about it.*

As much as I really need to talk to somebody, there's no way I can talk to Mom. I tried once when another challenging incident like this happened, only to be met with a total lack of response. Back then, I still had a glimmer of hope that she would be there for me, that she would support me. No more. While the disappointment at my inability to lean on her still lingers, I have come to resist needing my mother.

I slink home. As I walk through the door, as always, I scan Mom's face and her demeanor. I can feel a thick heaviness and a tense energy in the room before I even shut the door behind me. Mom has a nasty scowl on her face and her cigarette is just hanging off her lip. I take in the kitchen and notice that it's not cleaned up and organized, as it usually is when I get home. The radio is off—she's not listening to her favorite music. Uh-oh!

Mom's greeting further sets the tone. Some days it's loving and cheerful. Other days, like today, it's nonexistent. She barely even acknowledges that I have entered the room. Once again, there is no time for me to be consumed with my own issues right now. Instead, I need to try talking to her to see why she's so upset.

"Mom, what happened? What's wrong?" I ask.

"Never mind, never mind!"

"Are you sure?"

"Never mind, I said!" she repeats angrily.

"Do you want me to clean the dishes out of the sink?"

"No! Just get out of my hair."

I can't do anything to help Mom today. I exhale a sigh of relief as I walk up the stairs. For once I don't have to deal with her temperamental mood. Thank goodness. For a change I can take care of my needs instead of hers.

I escape to my room and close the door. I peel open the plastic wrapper on a brand-new cassette, load the tape into my boom box and lie down on my bed. As I listen to the music and wait for the radio DJ to play that new Madonna song so that I can record it and start making a new mix tape, I can start to feel myself unwind. I don't often get time like this for myself. I get lost in the music. It soothes me and provides me with a temporary escape from the incident at school, from my mom, from our stultifying home life.

I also have other ways to soothe myself. I love crawling under my bed just below the headboard to the large pile of loose change I've been collecting. Half-dollars, quarters, nickels, dimes and even some pennies are piled so high they almost reach the bottom of the box spring, the result of my collecting all the loose change I can find. My pile of coins is also the result of my creeping downstairs in the middle of the night to empty out Mom's change purse, which most of the time is filled to the top with nothing but quarters. This rapidly grows my secret money stash. I lie on my belly on the floor lining up the change into stacks of dollars. I have a total of five dollars and twenty-three cents. Wow, that's a lot of money. Tomorrow morning, if I leave for school just a little early, I can make it to Roots, the corner store just beyond my church, before school and buy myself a big bag of candy.

I wake up super-early the next morning and get out the door in fifteen minutes. I have to hurry if I want to get to Roots before first period begins. I practically run down First Street. When I finally get there, it's busy. Businessmen are getting their coffee before they catch their train across the street. I rush in the front door of the store and hustle around the side of the coffee counter. And there it is! Just in front of the cashier. Tiers and rows of any kind of candy imaginable. There must be over one hundred different types of candy, from chocolate bars to Twizzlers to rows of Hubba Bubba gum and Blow Pops. It's paradise. Overwhelmed, I try to figure out which candy to select. I stuff as many pieces of candy in my hands as I can and reach over the tiers to the counter so that I can pay. Then the cashier hands me a brown paper bag stuffed with Snickers bars, Milky Way bars, Zagnuts, Reese's Pieces and gummy bears.

As I head down the street toward school, I unwrap a Snickers bar and start eating it. It's so chocolaty and yummy and completely erases any stress at home or at school.

I love my little sugar-shopping sprees and I love that I have enough candy to last me the entire day. I'll be out of candy by the time I get home, but at that point I can hopefully jump on my bike and go for a ride after what I'm sure will be a dreadful day.

Fortunately, what was so traumatic for me yesterday is nonexistent today. My girlfriends meet me at school like nothing happened. They're already over yesterday's squabble, even though I clearly broke a social rule I didn't even know existed. I'm not introduced to these social mores at home, which means I'm always learning about them the hard way. But at least this situation has been resolved.

I'm going to keep my mouth shut from now on, I vow, determined not to risk losing my friends again.

The day has gone so well that I can't bear the idea of hanging out with Mom after school. I decide to see if I can make a break for it the second I get home. Mom seems to be in a good mood today and it's a beautiful spring day, so chances are good that she'll say yes.

I would never try this on a day when she's irritated and in a bad mood, but I don't always gauge the situation right. The other day when I asked to go for a ride, my Mom radar was off.

"No, young lady. Go to your room and do your homework. You should not be out roaming the streets. I want you in this house where you belong."

My fingers are crossed that today will be much different.

"Mom, can I go for a bike ride?" I ask.

"Yes, Michelle. I know you can't wait to get out of this house," Mom replies.

I throw on my play clothes and tear into the garage to grab my bike as quickly as I can before she changes her mind. Hopping on my bike while it's already moving, I fly down the driveway and onto the street. The breeze feels so good rushing through my hair as I ride as fast as I can to the corner. I relish the amazing sense of liberation I feel from school and the confines and negativity of my home life.

I ride all the way down Hyslip Avenue, a peaceful tree-lined neighborhood with beautifully landscaped homes, toward Knoll-wood Terrace. When I finally reach Tamaques Park, the streets are so quiet with barely any cars that I can ride my bike down the middle of the road with my hands in the air as I balance the bike between my legs. I'm so far from home now and it feels amazing. I turn back and head for Austin Street, where a few of my friends live, Bobby, Troy and Jenny. I stop off at Jenny's house.

Jenny and I sit on the front steps of their beautiful wrap-around porch. Their quaint house is situated on the bottom of an inclined street. Gorgeous yellow cloth awnings extend over each window, creating a congenial, cozy feeling. We hang out for a while talking about boys and school. Her mom finally calls her inside, so I leave. I know I'm supposed to get home, too, but no way. I don't want to go. I love this taste of liberty. So even though I know that I may get into big trouble for being out so long, I stay out and continue to ride.

Eventually I start to get chilly and realize the sun is going down.

Why didn't I think to grab a jacket? I think.

I keep riding for another twenty minutes or so. The smell of barbecues in the air from my neighbors grilling their dinners further reminds me that it's dinnertime. Mom will likely be pissed that I'm not home by now. Shoot, I really do have to go home.

By the time I ride my bike down the driveway to the big red garage door, I've been gone for a good three hours. Depending on what state Mom is in, she either won't care, or she will be home infuriated with me as she counts the minutes that have ticked by since my expected return. If it's the latter, there will surely be hell to pay for my brief taste of freedom.

I latch the garage door and head into the house. That's strange. Mom isn't in the kitchen cooking dinner. The kitchen is empty. I walk upstairs to find her passed out in her recliner, where she was watching TV.

"Hi, Mom," I say, knowing that the sound of my voice will wake her.

"Where have you been, young lady?" she replies groggily.

Shoot, I thought I was off the hook.

"I was just out riding. It's so nice outside. You know I love spring."

She doesn't respond.

"What's for dinner?" I ask in an attempt to redirect the conversation.

"When your father gets home, we'll get Chinese," she replies. "You better get that homework started."

And just like that it's over. She isn't nearly as angry as I feared. I just never know which mom I'm going to get.

CHAPTER 17

Awareness of My Own Needs

IT'S LONELY AT HOME TODAY. Dad had to cover the weekend shift, so he left early this morning. He used to take me bowling early on Saturday mornings. I just loved his undivided attention and getting to spend time with him, but it's been ages since we did that together.

It's a gloomy day outside—the clouds have created a gray sky. They say it's going to rain all day. I lie in bed watching Saturday morning cartoons on the small television that sits atop my dresser. I'm bored, but something else is wrong. I just can't tell what it is.

I go downstairs to get my cereal. Mom is crocheting in her chair, a broken-in plush floral armchair that is situated in the corner of the living room with a matching ottoman. Alongside that chair, which is exclusively reserved for her, sit white plastic shopping bags filled with craft supplies and yarn. She pulls an arm's length of yarn toward her before looking up.

"Good morning, Michelle," she says. Her disgusted tone alerts me that she's irritated this morning. I quickly get my bowl of cereal and retreat to my bedroom, consumed by a feeling of loneliness.

I often feel lonely. There's nobody to talk to at home now that my siblings have left. And I won't see my friends until Monday morning at school. I walk over to the giant pile of stuffed animals in the corner of my room and grab the biggest fluffy stuffed teddy bear in the pile. I close my eyes and squeeze him tight. Tears start coursing down my face, triggered by all-too-familiar feelings of not belonging in my own family.

Why am I here? I think. *Why am I not with my real mom? Why did she leave me?*

I wish I were an adult already, but that's so far away. Adults are the only ones who really matter. They're the only ones who can make decisions.

Why is life here so hard?

The reality of my daily life seems like it will go on forever. It's hard to look forward to a bright future when I'm so disconnected from who I really am and what my dreams are. My only value and purpose is to facilitate a bad situation at home, and I can't see past that.

At every opportunity, I'm reminded of how insignificant I am. Especially when I make mistakes. Yesterday after school I was hungry, so I made myself a snack. Unfortunately, I left some cracker crumbs behind. Mom yelled at me for making a mess and not cleaning up after myself.

"Michelle, you're nothing but a snot-brat slob," she screamed in fury.

Her cruel words have really been pissing me off lately. Out of anger, I responded.

"Relax, it was just a cracker crumb."

"Don't you ever talk back to me, young lady! Just who the hell do you think you are?"

Before I could even apologize, she slapped me full force across my mouth with the back of her hand. No matter how old

I get, she continues to hit me. I despise that. I'm not a little kid anymore. Why does she have to keep hitting me?

Mom was not done with me.

"Wait until your father gets home. He'll deal with you then," she yelled. "Now go to your room!"

When Dad came home from work, visibly tired, he said very little and sat right down at the head of the dinner table to eat. As Mom served him, she told him about what happened.

"And this one was quite a pig today," she said, pointing her finger at me. "She decided to make a mess all over the clean kitchen countertop when she got home from school! As if I have nothing better to do than to clean up after her."

I sat quietly listening to her recount what happened.

"And then this smart ass goes and mouths off," she continued. "That is it! She's grounded for a week. I'm sick of her talking back in this house."

"But I really didn't say anything wrong," I chimed in. This only further irritated her. I tried to continue with my defense, but Dad interrupted me.

"Your mother said you're grounded. Period. When are you going to listen? End of discussion."

While Mom always threatens, Dad rarely intervenes in disciplining me now that I'm older. Mom is the one who dictates how things go and how the house will run. Dad has become the reinforcing parent, with Mom making him out to be someone I should fear. He always backs her no matter how crazy the situation. While he never hits me, I'm afraid of his stern words.

I find myself trying hard to avoid him, but suddenly it seems like he's stalking me so that he can catch me doing something wrong like hanging out with boys. When he does, he always embarrasses me, which usually compromises my relationships. These boys, who really like me, give me their affection and attention, both of which I crave, especially considering how little of either I get from Dad.

There is less and less conversation between Dad and me. In fact, there's very little connection at all. I can vaguely remember crawling up on his lap and getting the best hugs from him when I was younger. I really miss that. I would give anything to talk to and connect with him. I will later learn that he's the one person who could relate to my situation with Mom more than anyone else, since he grew up with his own abusive mother. Unfortunately, that exchange is not something I ever experience at home. On the flip side, Grandma is as nice to me as she was mean to my father. Thankfully, I can get away to her house, the one place where I can get all the affection and attention I need.

CHAPTER 18

Grandma's Love

FOR AS LONG AS I CAN REMEMBER, I always enjoyed visiting my grandma at the little house she relocated to in Iselin, New Jersey. But I was sad when Grandma and Pop-Pop moved from their perfect farmhouse in the woods in upstate New York.

After a four-hour ride, we would finally arrive at their quaint house situated in the trees on acres of land far away from any neighbors. I loved everything about being there, from the giant swing on the front porch to the large hill in the backyard that we would toboggan down in the wintertime, making sure to avoid the manure barrel that Pop-Pop kept for his garden. In the fall, I loved picking apples off the tree and currants from the currant bush in the backyard. I can still smell Grandma's apple pies cooling on the window-lined porch that overlooked the beautiful fields behind their house where the deer would roam.

The nooks and crannies in an old farmhouse are a joy for a youngster to explore—each doorway opened to a new room and space perfect for a small child. Fetching jugs of fresh milk and eggs early in the morning at Sluggers Farm, a smelly place filled with cats, was always the highlight of visiting Grandma and Pop-Pop.

It's been a while now since Pop-Pop passed away. I loved him and miss him so much. I can still smell his cigar, and remember sitting on his lap when I was younger. I think about him a lot. He was the first family member I ever lost. His funeral was so hard for me. Losing him makes me treasure Grandma even more.

While Grandma's house in Iselin certainly doesn't compare to the farmhouse, at least she lives much closer to us so now we can visit her more frequently. As I walk through the front of her cozy house, a faint scent of her perfume lingers from when she was dressing earlier to go out with her girlfriend Rose. From the feminine floral couch and drapery in her living room to her well-attended garden lining the back deck just adjacent to her covered swing, Grandma's house is a wonderful reflection of her.

Grandma is a beautiful woman and the classiest lady I have ever met. She has soft silver hair and beautiful blue eyes. When she smiles, her beautiful blue eyes squint in such a sweet way. She takes great pride in her appearance with her hair always done and her makeup always perfectly applied. When she's all dressed up to go out, every detail about her is just perfect. If she's wearing slacks, there's not one wrinkle, and her beautiful blouses are always so soft and feminine.

We usually take the thirty-minute drive to see her just after finishing dinner. Grandma greets us at the front door with a wine glass in hand. She loves her wine and beer. You will always find her with an ice-cold glass of beer or a chilled chardonnay nearby. That's her guilty pleasure.

When we go to Grandma's house, she always has something freshly baked waiting for us in her kitchen. Being in her kitchen, which is half carpeted and half tiled, with her dark oak dining room table situated on the carpeted space, has me feeling that I'm in the heart of her home. It's a simple kitchen with minimal appliances, yet she has everything she needs to turn out the most amazing dinners and wonderful desserts.

It's always a great surprise to see what she's made. Today, I find a yummy apple pie cooling on the kitchen table. Perched on top of the golden-brown crust is a little ceramic black bird that she uses to help let the pie vent during baking. I can't wait to dig into that when she makes coffee later.

After we have coffee and apple pie, Mom and Dad go next door to visit with my Aunt Muriel. Grandma and I sit down on the living room couch to watch TV.

Grandma has a way of making me feel so special and like I'm her very favorite granddaughter. She's the one person I can really talk to about what goes on at home.

"So how is Mom?" she asks me.

"Okay," I respond. I reflect for a moment and then repeat, "She's doing okay. Not good. Just okay."

Using my hands, I visually show her. "So, on the roller coaster, she's about midway from the top headed down for another decline again. Dad and I are trying to help her stay up, but that's not easy. She cries now and then. I know that if I'm a good girl she won't be sad. I'm trying my very best to make her happy when she's sad."

It's nice to be able to talk about Mom's illness so freely. This is usually a secret. But Grandma knows and understands about Mom.

"How are you doing?" she asks me.

Nobody but Grandma and Aunt Muriel ever really asks me that. Unlike some of my other aunts, my Aunt Muriel—my father's sister and my very dear godmother—has always been very loving and supportive.

I have to stop and think about how I'm feeling. I have learned to put on my facade and mask any needs I may have. After all, I'm not sick. I'm okay. So taking time to consider my own emotions feels downright strange and uncomfortable.

I could tell her about Mom's last manic episode when she went from crying to getting really mad and slapping me across the mouth, or how I continuously have to hide her illness from my close friends. Instead I say, "School is good. I'm doing much better in algebra now. And my best friend, Katie, invited me to her birthday party; I can't wait to go."

I keep the conversation innocuous just like I always do. My feelings and needs are unimportant.

Just last week, I sat in my dad's truck with him before he dropped me off at school, strategizing about how to care for Mom and her crying. I'm exhausted from all of her crying and her emotional highs and lows. All I want to do is cry and scream at the same time. I want to tell my dad that I'm the one in need of a hug and that this is all too much for me. But I can't. I have to suppress how I'm feeling. I've grown accustomed to being a chameleon and just showing up as what others need me to be.

In a weird way, this helps me to feel accepted. My entire identity has become about taking care of my mom and riding that emotional roller coaster with her at the expense of being authentically myself and true to my own needs—just when I'm trying to figure out who I am as a young teenager.

In the absence of any kind of home support, and too few visits to Grandma, I turn to boys, a lot of boys, whose eyes and attention I catch. Over the next few years, my dependence on male attention and affection will only grow. They provide solace and both a mental and physical escape.

In hindsight, I realize I was so young, but I needed them. I needed attention and affection from somewhere. This became my lifeline.

CHAPTER 19

Reveling in the Attention From a Boy

M Y LAST CLASS ENDS, and I rush to my locker.

Is he going to meet me today? I wonder.

Nate is so cute with his short brown hair and adorable dimples when he smiles at me. He is all I can think about all day long. In math class, I can't focus at all. Instead of paying attention to the assignment, I draw hearts with his initials on my brown-bag book cover and think about his smile. Then in social studies, I find myself doodling in my notebook. *MD + NA*, I write.

At the end of the school day, I look up from packing my backpack and there he is at my locker. My heart skips a beat. He is here for me. I get to walk home from school with him today. I'm so excited.

We walk down the street from the school. I giggle the entire way at the funny stories he's telling me. As we approach the wooded area near my house, he holds my hand and kisses my cheek. I get goose bumps all over and my heart sinks to my stomach.

He is going to kiss me for real, I think.

We stop at the big oak tree in the middle of the woods. He stares into my eyes and I can't stop smiling. This feeling of being completely adored is intoxicating. The woods are quiet and dark. It's peaceful and private here. He leans in and kisses me just like in the romantic soap operas I watch with my mother when I'm home from school. My body tingles all over. I never want this feeling to end. Then, he brushes a piece of hair out of my eyes. I feel like a princess—my prince is sweeping me away from my turbulent life. For a brief moment, I even feel comfortable in my own skin.

What a difference from just last night at tap-dancing class. Forced to look in the oversized mirrors, I had seen an insecure, sad girl staring down at her feet trying to get the steps right, which only earned me a reprimand from my teacher, Mrs. Joan.

"Michelle, stop staring down at your feet and look up. You can't stare at your feet during the recital in a few short weeks. We need to see your face."

She always reminds me to raise my head, watch myself in the mirrors and smile. In this moment with Nate, I don't have to be told to have confidence and smile. It's effortless.

He kisses me again. I revel in it. I don't want this moment to end. When I open my eyes, reality abruptly shows up. The sun has started to go down and the air has cooled.

Shoot, it's getting late.

I know I have to get home. Now. The repercussions for me being this late are going to be significant. Still, it's been so worth it. After a long romantic kiss goodbye, I begin my walk home from the woods, smiling from ear to ear and totally enamored.

I reach my house and take a big, deep breath before entering. I'm only forty-five minutes late.

What's the big deal, anyway? I think.

I know the rules. I also know that not one of my friends has to deal with what I do at home. It's totally unfair. It's not like I was off committing a crime. I was just hanging out with my boyfriend. Why is my mother so controlling and domineering? I hate it.

Mom greets me at the door.

"Where the hell have you been, young lady?" she yells.

"I was held after school for something," I respond.

Really, Michelle, I think. *You couldn't have thought of a better excuse than that on your way home from school? You idiot!*

"When are you going to learn? You're grounded!" Mom screams. "Go to your room right now."

Oh, man. Why is she so mean? I won't be able to see Nate tomorrow after school. She's going to watch my every single move now! I hate this.

I head to my room, wishing I was older.

When I grow up, I can't wait to leave here and be on my own, I think. *I will have the most freedom and happiness ever.*

I can't wait.

As frustrating as it is to be in trouble yet again, I'm still high on that kiss from Nate. I'm going to make him a mix tape of my favorite songs. I pull out a cassette tape and put it into my boom box. As I lie on my bed waiting for the right songs to come on the radio, I doodle his name on my notebook. I should be doing algebra homework, but I can't stop thinking about Nate. Just then, my favorite Air Supply love song plays on the radio. Quickly I hit the record button.

Hold me in your arms for just another day.

I promise this one will go slow.

We have the right you know.

We have the right you know.

Here I am, the one that you love, asking for another day.
Understand the one that you love loves you in so many ways.

The lyrics are perfect for how I'm feeling about Nate. These feelings are a welcomed distraction from the upset I would normally be feeling because of my mother's anger and sickness. For now, I don't have to focus on—and strategize about—how to get Mom well. I focus on him instead.

I'll be back at school and will see his face soon enough, I think.

For now, I'll just dream about him and imagine what it will be like to see him again. That way I won't have to feel the present moment.

CHAPTER 20

My CYO

Lᴵꜰᴇ ᴀᴛ ʜᴏᴍᴇ ʀᴇᴍᴀɪɴꜱ ᴛᴏᴜɢʜ. As a young teen, I still have to hold everything together at home. I don't get a reprieve from playing the role of a nurse to my sick mom. I constantly put her life in front of my own and parent my own parent at the exclusion of my own life.

When I finally return to school after being out again for another two weeks to care for Mom, my friend Jenny approaches me as soon as I reach my locker.

"Are you okay?" she asks, looking me dead in the face.

"Yes. I was just really, really sick. It was a nasty cold. I'm feeling better, though."

I can tell she's suspicious. I look away from her eyes. I'm not ready to deal with telling anyone else that Mom was down for the count again and that I needed to take care of her. I just want the whole situation to go away. It's hard enough dealing with the fact that she's now at the mental hospital. I sure don't need to tell anyone about that. They will judge me and my family.

As I walk into my next class, I overhear a conversation outside the classroom doorway just moments before the bell rings.

"It's going to be awesome!" Chris says.

"Is Gilrain going?" Tom asks Jeremy.

"Yes, and so are Kim and Pat," Jeremy responds.

Sounds like another gathering at Tom's house after school.

Nobody ever tells me or invites me to these gatherings.

That stinks, I think. *Tom only lives two blocks from my house and these are my classmates and friends.*

I quickly blink back the tears of disappointment.

Oh, stop it, Michelle, I say to myself. *You know you don't really want to go anyway.*

The truth is that I wouldn't feel comfortable hanging out with them. I still struggle finding a place where I fit in. I haven't found it at school or at home. So I don't feel comfortable anywhere.

That changes when Timmy, a former grammar school classmate of mine, mentions that he's going on a ski trip this weekend with Catholic Youth Organization (CYO) from our church.

"It's the Catholic teen group formed with my church, Holy Trinity," he says. "Joel, Cindy and Terri are all going."

I know these kids from elementary school. I haven't seen them in years. My faith just hasn't been that prominent in my life since leaving Catholic school after the fifth grade. With all that is going on at home, I barely even say my prayers at night and I rarely make it to church on Sunday.

"Really?" I say.

"Yes. We're all getting on the bus tonight after dinner."

I wish I were going. It would be great to hang out with them all again.

It doesn't take long for me to learn more about CYO. The group meets on Wednesday nights just above the gymnasium of my former Catholic school in a space they call The Lighthouse.

With my parents' consent, I decide to go to the next meeting.

Mom drops me off in front of the school at 7:00 p.m. On the door, a handwritten note reads: *CYO tonight at 7:15 p.m.—Upstairs in The Lighthouse.*

I walk up the small stairwell to The Lighthouse. When I get to the top of the stairwell, I find another door with a small glass window. I peek through and see what looks like someone's comfortable living room that's nothing like my old sterile Catholic school classroom in the adjacent building. Chestnut-colored carpeting canvases the room and a large wooden cross hangs on the wall below the clock. I open the door and enter the large recreational space. Straight ahead of me, a few kids are playing pool. I've never played pool before. I thought that was reserved only for adults. It looks like they're having fun.

I want to learn, I think.

I begin to scope out the setting in my usual way. Mom has unwittingly trained me to assess the vibe and feel of every room I enter. As I look around, I start to absorb the energy and demeanor of the kids in the room. In the corner, I spot a girl reclined on a comfy couch with her feet up. She's reading a book and twirling her hair. Nobody is telling her to put her feet down. A handsome older boy walks over to the mahogany end table next to the girl reading. With a loud squish, he then plops down in the cushy chair next to her.

A collection of records, including an old John Denver album, on the coffee table tells me there must be a record player here somewhere.

Wait, they listen to John Denver?

I really like the sound of his voice. At home we don't have his records, nor do I have my own turntable.

I bet I could listen to that record whenever I wanted to here.

Just the thought of hearing John Denver's warm voice and sitting on that comfy couch makes me feel at ease.

This living room space feels quite different than our dark living room, which is smoky from all the cigarettes. As opposed to the depressing heaviness at home, this Lighthouse gathering place feels light and comfortable. It's not overly immaculate like our house is sometimes. Nor is it too messy like our house is sometimes. It's tidy, yet feels lived in. I feel good being here and that makes me want to stay for a while.

Laughter from the far corner of the room catches my attention. I follow it into a small kitchen with a table and a few chairs. As I approach, I can see several kids congregating with a priest and giggling uncontrollably.

I step through the doorway into the kitchen.

"Hi," I say, surprising myself. "I'm here for CYO tonight."

"Yes, we're about to get started," the priest says. "What's your name?"

"I'm Michelle."

"Welcome. I'm Father Rich Kelly. They call me Duck."

With that, everyone in the kitchen smiles and tells me their names. A few moments later, Father Kelly gets up and directs everyone to the main recreation area. The moment Father Kelly walks into the main room, I observe his gait, or should I say waddle, and immediately see how he earned his nickname.

Many familiar faces greet me as I walk in.

"Hi, Michelle!" Tanya says.

"Hey, Michelle," Cindy says.

"Michelle, what's up?" Billy says.

I immediately feel welcome. Still, I retain a level of skepticism—I don't know everyone I'm seeing. There are still so many new faces in this group.

We all grab a space on the floor and sit Indian style, forming a circle around a small worn-out living room chair upon which Father Kelly is seated. He moves to the very edge of the chair so he can join hands with the kids in the circle. The rest of us bow our heads as the room gets really quiet.

Father Kelly starts to pray.

"Lord Jesus, let all gathered here tonight know that we do so in your name. Thank you for giving us the chance to teach our faith to each other through our actions. Grant us personal acceptance of the dignity of all individuals. And, above all, let us in all things demonstrate a spirit of love and respect for all."

Love and respect for all? That sure doesn't happen in my house.

After reading a few passages from the Bible, Father Kelly begins talking to us about the scripture. He asks the group a few questions. I sit quietly just observing the interactions, some of which are funny and some of which are serious.

Being here feels better and better as the evening goes on. Strangers smile at me. I feel warmth from others. Something is different about this group. And something is different about me. I'm comfortable in this space.

Wow! I think. *Maybe I have found my spot.*

Over the next few weeks and months, I feel more and more at home with this group. Mom allows me to be here as much as I like. It's strange to have so much freedom to be with this group. We meet weekly for Bible study and then again on Sundays for open gym sessions where we play pool, watch a movie, listen to music or play basketball in the gym. It's fun to be able to just hang out on Sunday nights with Father Kelly and the other kids.

Even so, I can't let myself get too comfortable. I remind myself not to let my guard down. Even though it feels good being here, I need to be careful.

I can't let them know the real me. I can't let them know what's going on at home. I can't let them know my secret.

I remain cautious even as I realize that I don't need to make them laugh or share gossip about other kids for them to like me.

It's odd that they seem to already like me. I try hard to resist the sense of safety, which feels so unfamiliar.

I begin to connect. For the first time in my life, I finally understand what it's like to be part of a group and what it means to be fully accepted for just being myself. I no longer feel small, insignificant or not enough, like I'm used to feeling at home and in school. I get acceptance, warmth and genuine support from this group.

As time goes on, I realize that what you see is what you get here. During Bible study meetings, I witness kids sharing their fears, their tears and their hearts with the group. They're rewarded with generously shared hugs of love.

Several months later, I find myself on a spiritual and very emotional retreat weekend during which my bond with this group only deepens. There is a genuine vulnerability that shows up during these weekends. I have never experienced this before. The talks given by the older members of the group make me cry and make me realize that this has now really become my safe space.

I feel like this group is my extended family. At home, when things get hard and I'm feeling sad or down, I know I will feel better just coming to The Lighthouse. Being around this group and Father Kelly just has a way of helping me feel okay.

Before I know it, I'm asked to give my own talk at the upcoming retreat weekend. I realize giving my talk will mean being vulnerable and authentically sharing myself just as I have witnessed others do in their talks. It will mean telling my secret about what life is like at home for me. I've never shared this with a large group before. Even though I feel like this is a safe space, I don't know how I'm going to actually share my story.

What will I say? I think as I sit down and begin writing my message. *What do I want to share?*

That's when it hits me. I will talk about the most meaningful lessons I've learned growing up with my mom. So I write my talk and color my poster for my upcoming presentation.

Then comes the big weekend.

Retreats are a big deal in my CYO, with many kids attending from all over the community. As many as a hundred kids sign up for this magical three-day experience. On Friday night, in front of The Lighthouse, sleeping bags in hand, we all load up on the yellow school bus and head to our retreat center in Lebanon, New Jersey.

After a quick sixty-minute bus ride, I find myself at a beautiful camp tucked deep in the woods. Adjacent to the large main hall, I find two smaller cabins. The girls' cabin has two sets of sleeping bunks with bathrooms and showers situated on either end of the building and a community space in the center adorned with inviting couches and an oversized fireplace. Below the main hall down a small dirt road, an outdoor chapel with a stone altar and rows of stone pews surrounded by evergreen trees has been built into the side of a mountain. The pine needles serve as a soft carpet beneath my feet.

When I head to the main hall that night, the sky is pitch black. I stop long enough to realize that it's totally peaceful and quiet. Even better, because the area is so remote, there are no highway lights or streetlights to take away from the tranquility and bright twinkling stars. The only light comes from the top of a small hill just behind the main hall, where a thirty-foot-high cross that appears to be magically illuminated shines brightly.

It's not long before I realize how meaningful this space will be for me. We spend hours that night sitting in a circle on the main hall's large heated floors holding hands in group prayer and singing together. We spend more time praying, talking and growing even closer as we share warm cups of hot cocoa.

Before I know it, Saturday morning arrives. Today is the big day.

The large group is seated in groups of eight at large round tables in the oversized main recreation room. In the corner of the room is a small stage with a podium, upon which the speaker has hung a beautiful nature poster. She speaks openly about her struggle with cancer, and when she finishes, the room is filled with tears. She's a strong survivor who is adored by everyone.

How can I give my talk? I think. *It's so insignificant compared with hers.*

I sit nervously at one of the tables. My stomach spins and my hands are clammy.

Finally, it's my turn. I'm introduced and invited to the podium. I approach the small stage and tape my poster to the podium. When I look out to the sea of faces in the audience all looking up at me, I get this sick feeling in the pit of my stomach.

Overwhelmed, I look at Father Kelly standing in the back of

the room. He smiles and nods at me. That reassurance gives me the little bit of encouragement that I need.

I begin to share.

"My mother is quite sick. She struggles with something called bipolar disorder. Bipolar disorder is a mood disorder that causes her to be depressed sometimes. It also causes her to be very nervous and anxious, too. I love my mom so much. But sometimes being around her is like a roller coaster. Some days she's up and some days she's down. When she's really sick, it's hard for me to deal with. Sometimes she has to go away to the hospital and I can't see her until we are able to visit with her. I really hate not having my mom."

Suddenly, tears overwhelm me. I start thinking about having to go to that hospital to see my own mother. It's just so unfair.

I'm now crying at the podium—in front of everyone. I have just shared my deepest secret with them.

Ugh, what have I done?

Somehow, I'm able to pull myself together and get through my entire talk.

"Most people have no idea what I'm dealing with at home," I say. "They only know what they see on the surface. Always remember that we never really know what others are dealing with. We should try hard to be kind to everyone."

I look out over that sea of faces. "Thank you," I conclude as I end my talk.

Applause unlike anything I've ever heard before erupts. It's for me! Several members of the retreat planning team come up to the podium and hug me. I begin to cry again. A profound sense of relief consumes me. Regardless of my apprehension to share myself, I've shared my secret and my revelation has been met with nothing but love and acceptance.

A flood of *palancas* follows later that day. In Spanish, *palanca* means lever, and it symbolizes that, like a lever, it has enabled a person to move something that's normally beyond their strength. After each talk, the group is given an opportunity to write a *palanca* to the speaker in the form of a small hand written note.

The outpouring of love and support only deepens my connection with the group. As I read each of these *palancas*, I'm further grounded in the love and support these people have for me. The *palancas*, from my closest CYO friends and total strangers alike, offer encouragement and such positive messages.

I recognize that not only has a massive burden finally been lifted from my shoulders, I have found a fulfilling space of acceptance and love, so I no longer have to search for either.

Everything is really going to be okay.

CHAPTER 21

Getting Away

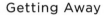

MY SENSE OF REPRIEVE DOESN'T last nearly as long as I would like. By age seventeen, I no longer can stand being at home. I do everything I can to stay away. I request more hours at work. I take on any extracurricular activities that I can. I become an athletic trainer for our sports teams, wrapping their ankles and wrists before games.

I will do anything not to be there more than I absolutely have to.

Thank God I have a part-time restaurant job. That fills a ton of hours and I often have to work super-late. Unlike what I get at home, here they appreciate me and give me a lot of positive feedback for my hard work and contribution. The appreciation from my customers and managers is a welcome escape from the chaos I know I'll encounter at home with Mom.

Those long hours at the restaurant lead to my falling in love with the owner's son, Brian. He often runs the restaurant for his father and has to work long hours as well.

It's fun getting to work with Brian, especially since we often have to stay late. At the end of the night when the restaurant is slow, we get to hang out in the tiny restaurant office together. Before long, we start dating. After six months, he asks me to his senior prom. My senior year is about to finish up. Instead of focusing on college, I have to turn my attention homeward.

Once again, things are starting to fall apart and I'm exhausted from dealing with Mom's emotional instability. I'm exhausted from repeatedly picking up the pieces at home and always cleaning the house. My once-appreciated hard work at home has become a job as thankless as it is expected.

After all the years and all the different drugs, doctor appointments and hospital visits, you would think that Mom would be getting better. But she's not. She's getting worse and I'm less and less able to manage her delusional states.

Looking back, it's no wonder. Mom clearly was dealing with bipolar psychosis. I know that now. All I knew then was that life with her was suddenly getting harder.

I walk into the living room. It's six o'clock. Mom clearly has not made a move to the kitchen. Our breakfast dishes are still on the counter from this morning. She's sitting in her armchair staring out into space just chain-smoking. She appears very disconnected and out of it, as if she's not really there. As a result, I discount her presence.

"Looks like I have to figure out dinner once again," I mumble under my breath.

She hasn't even been to the grocery store in weeks. I wonder to myself if there is anything in the refrigerator that I can even make.

I will later learn that when someone experiences bipolar psychosis, they remain totally coherent even when they're partly there and partly not. Mom has no problem abruptly reminding me of that.

"What did you just say, young lady?" she exclaims. "This house is a filthy mess, Michelle! I want to know when the hell you're going to make time for your chores like you do for your other activities!"

Tonight she's yelling at me for not cleaning the kitchen and the rest of our home. This morning she was furious with me for forgetting to take out the trash with its stinky Chinese food remains.

Her nastiness elevates. This time, so does mine. I have had enough. I'm so sick of feeling totally powerless and trapped. I'm sick of feeling like I can't breathe in my own home.

"Well, excuse me for working and being responsible!" I shout.

I know what I'm doing and what will follow. But I don't care. For a moment in time, I'm no longer the complacent Michelle who always agrees with Mom in order to avoid a confrontation and beatings.

Mom quickly rushes over to me. She corners me up against the kitchen sink. She starts slapping my mouth repeatedly with both her hands.

"What did you just say to me? What the hell did you just say to me?" she shouts.

Her lips are tight and her eyes are bulging. I can't even get a word out because the force of her slapping my face has knocked the wind out of me.

This beating wounds unlike any other I've gotten, not because of the aggressive force of her backhand but because of the ruthlessness and complete disrespect she's demonstrating toward me. I'm not a little kid anymore.

Even as she pounds on me, I can see how every day I've avoided being at home has added to the fury brewing within her. Now all that pent-up anger is being released on me. After all these years, I still don't understand how someone who loves you can inflict such emotional and physical pain.

That's it! I have had it.

Instead of sitting there crying my eyes out, and feeling powerless and sorry for myself like I usually do, I grab my duffel bag, fill it with my things and run out the door. From a friend's house down the street, I call Brian. Within minutes he picks me up and takes me to his father's place, where he lives.

"I'm done. I never want to go back there!" I scream. "I hate them. I hate that house. I hate my life."

"It's okay. We can get an apartment. Why don't we?" he asks me.

"Okay," I say. "Let's do it!"

I explain the entire story to Brian's dad and stepmother. His stepmom leans into me and wraps her arms around me. His dad rubs my back and then offers to call my parents.

"No! I don't want to ever see them again. I hate them."

They can tell that I'm drained. I'm as white as the tip of Mom's cigarette. I don't even have enough energy to move myself off the couch. The impact that my tumultuous life at home has had on me is evident. I can't stop trembling.

I gratefully spend that night at Brian's father's house, safe in Brian's arms. Within weeks, he and I get our own apartment and I move in. My parents are not happy with me, but I don't care. I have finally gotten out. I'm done being controlled and manipulated by them. I'm done being the housewife and housekeeper for them.

I love our little one-bedroom apartment and the complete freedom I finally have. Located on the third floor of a large Victorian home, there's a small eat-in kitchen to the left of the apartment's front door, with large windows that overlook a small parking lot behind the home, and a tiny bedroom and weathered bathroom to the right. Straight ahead from the main hallway is the living room with a larger picture window and a cozy seat beneath. In the wintertime, I sit there and feel the wind coming through the poorly insulated windowpanes, and it doesn't matter a bit. I adore this perfect little apartment.

Even though most of the time I'm in the apartment alone because Brian is always working, I enjoy the peace and quiet. We don't have much furniture, but we have a kitchen and a dining table, so I can cook us dinner. And I don't mind that our mattress is on the bedroom floor. Despite our attempts to economize and all the extra shifts we take at the restaurant, however, money is tight. It's hard trying to work, eat and pay $500 in rent. Before long, we're unable to make our payments and are told to move out.

Ever since leaving my family, I've dreaded more than anything the idea of having to move back home. Back into the dysfunctional life I ran away from. Now that's exactly where I'm headed. With my few belongings all packed, I wait for my parents to come pick me up and take me back home.

I can't believe I have to go back there. I hate this!

Mom and Dad arrive at my apartment. When I meet them on the front porch, they each give me a big hug and a kiss. Mom gets teary-eyed at the sight of me. Her hug is extra-long.

They're being much nicer to me than ever before, I think.

It really seems like they've missed me.

Maybe this time will be different.

As we pull into the driveway, my stomach starts to twist at the sight of the house. All the bad memories from the last time

I was home come rushing back. I feel suffocated and we haven't even gotten out of the car. I quickly ignore the feelings, something I've become so very good at doing.

We walk in the back door carrying my stuff. Although the house appears clean and neat, it feels a little different. I head up the hallway stairs. When I reach my bedroom, I notice the walls are yellowish brown. In all the years I've lived in this bedroom, I don't remember them being that color.

I take a damp tissue from my pocket and rub a small space on the wall, revealing the bright white plaster beneath. The years of cigarette smoking have stained the walls, even in my room. It's disgusting. Before unpacking, I decide to clean every wall using water and pure bleach.

Later that evening, we sit down to have dinner together.

"Young lady, you're going to have to start paying rent. You also need to pay the garbage pickup bill each month."

Great, I think. *I get to pay rent, pay for the trash and I get to clean the house.*

"And, if you want to go out, you can, but the doors will be locked at 10:00 p.m. every night," Mom says. "If you're not home by then, you'll need to find someplace to stay for the night."

I suddenly realize that nothing has really changed. Instead, the conditions at home have actually worsened.

That suffocating feeling returns yet again, especially because conditions at home are further compounded by summer ending and the reality that I now have to start classes at my local community college. I dread this. I know it will merely be an extension of high school all over again.

Why won't Mom and Dad support my dream of going to the College of St. Elizabeth? It seems like the perfect school for me. I can still remember the devastation that I felt when they wouldn't even allow me to apply.

"Mom, look, I got the brochure for the College of St. Elizabeth. Doesn't the campus look beautiful? It says that it's perfect for students who need just a little extra support."

Since my guidance counselor has just told my parents that, I think this is the perfect selling point. I'm filled with enthusiasm as I share the brochure with her. I can picture myself on the grounds of the campus as I look at the photos of the open brochure.

"Oh, you aren't going there for that kind of money! They're crazy with those prices. There's a perfectly good community college just a few miles away and that's where you're going. I'm not paying those high private school costs again," Mom announces, referring to the years I attended Holy Trinity Catholic school.

"But Mom, I really want to go there. I really miss being in Catholic school. I know that this will be a good school for me. I promise I'll work hard."

"You're crazy, young lady. The tuition is too high. Community college will be just fine."

Her curt response tells me that the conversation has ended.

As expected, life at community college sucks. All my friends are away at great colleges located far, far from our town. I envy them. This college I'm at is for idiots who couldn't get into a good school.

Classes at community college are far from intellectually stimulating. Not only are they boring, I have no interest in what's being taught. The social scene is equally dreadful, with all the people I dreaded seeing in high school back in class with me all over again. I hate it even more than I thought I would. As a result, it doesn't even serve as the escape from home that high school once did. And since Brian and I are no longer together, that distraction has disappeared as well.

Shortly after the first semester begins, I drop out. My parents are pissed because of the money they've spent on my classes. Although it's a fraction of what the school I really wanted to go to costs, they're still annoyed at me for quitting school. I would have never dropped out of the school that I really wanted to go to. Instead, I just know I would have flourished and done really well. I know I would have met some amazing new friends and really enjoyed my experience.

Even though my decision to drop out of college leaves both my parents quite frustrated, shortly thereafter my father offers to help me secure a temporary job at IBM. I agree because I know if I can get it, I will be paid much better than at the restaurant and the hours will be more stable. So off I go to interview for my first professional job at IBM.

Before long, I'm working as one of the only female technicians at IBM. Despite having no prior experience, I learn quickly from the other technicians who take me under their wing as well as from the repair training materials that they give me. I'm warmly embraced there. Along the way, many of my father's co-workers and friends become my new social group. I feel important being a part of my father's inner work circle.

I also appreciate that Dad and I get to have coffee and even lunch together on occasion. That one-on-one time away from home becomes special to me, especially because I'm finally impressing Dad again with all that I'm able to do at work. The praise and recognition I get from peers and my customers reflects positively on him. Suddenly I'm his good little girl again and I love it.

While this helps my relationship with Dad a great deal, the challenges we face at home with Mom do not change. She's going downhill once again. It looks like she's going to have to return to the hospital. While I hate her being so hard to manage at home, I hate the thought of her in the hospital even more.

CHAPTER 22

I Married My Mother

THANK GOODNESS FOR MY JOB AT IBM. My unsettled and turbulent home life makes me truly treasure my work life. And, as luck would have it, within the first six months there, I meet Chad, one of my father's colleagues. A tall and thin man with light brown hair and brown eyes, he's a very conservative, quiet, even-tempered and overly polite man from Pennsylvania. There's no drama with him.

Before long, we start dating, which I decide to share with my parents. I can immediately tell that Dad likes him. Mom and Dad don't seem to mind that I spend weeknights and weekends at his house down the shore.

I don't know what has caused them to have a change of heart, but I'm not going to question it because, between work and being with Chad, I'm barely home. Hallelujah!

After months of dating, we get engaged. I'm so excited, in part because I realize this will be my permanent out! We agree to get an apartment together, which finally allows me to leave my overbearing and suffocating house for good. Sure, I can go back and visit my parents if I want to, but my every move will no longer be controlled.

About a year later, Chad and I get married. Within months of our wedding, things start to get strange. My own husband begins to show those same familiar signs of depression and anxiety I witnessed with Mom.

"What is wrong?" I ask. "You seem upset. Is something bothering you?"

"Nothing's wrong. Leave me alone," he replies.

I don't believe it, so I ask him again.

"Why do you seem so distant and upset?"

"I'm just out of it! Leave it alone. I'm fine."

And that's how the routine goes. He becomes reclusive and distant, shutting me out entirely. We live in isolation while he contends with whatever he's dealing with all alone.

Compounding his change in mood is his newly overbearing and controlling manner. Suddenly, he wants me to always be at home with him. Since my going out with friends angers him, I find myself declining invitations just to avoid an upset with him. I feel increasingly isolated.

Marriage had seemed like an escape from my own controlling parents, something that would afford me the independence I yearned for. However, this marriage has turned out to be even more restricted and confining than life with my parents.

Fortunately, the survival skills I learned out of necessity start to really come in handy for me. Pulling myself up by my bootstraps is something I've known how to do from a very young age. My technician job launches me into a career where I'm able to acquire valuable skills and build my resume so I can advance myself.

My progress, however, is impeded by the scars I carry from how I've grown up. My self-esteem remains weak and is quickly diminished when Chad talks down to me, which he does more and more, and dismisses my new job as a senior-level secretary. His degrading insinuations are the worst.

"Did you take dictation today?" he asks in his smug voice, inferring that I sexually took care of my boss.

How can he talk to his own wife in such a deplorable manner?

As the months pass, he makes sure to constantly remind me of my lack of education and how sharply this contrasts with his Penn State degree. Even though I'm in an entirely different environment, those all-too-familiar feelings of worthlessness surface again.

How did this happen?

PART 3
Transformation

CHAPTER 23

Reclaiming My Life

MY MARRIAGE AND OUR HOME, where I once sought refuge from my own parents, has quickly turned into an exact mirror of the toxic dynamics I hated as a child. This time I no longer tolerate being made to feel less than I am, and find myself taking the necessary and painful steps to leave the relationship and ultimately divorce him. For the first time, I'm standing up for myself and reclaiming my life.

Leaving my marriage is different than leaving my parents. This time I'm not running away merely to escape. This time I have clarity and the first glimmer of the kind of life I want and know I deserve. I'm not exactly sure where or how I will find that life, but I'm incredibly clear that this isn't what I want.

The only way I'm going to live a life that makes me happy is to get out as quickly as possible, which means abandoning everything and boldly walking away from our home and our shared assets. Finally, I'm sticking up for myself and for my happiness. I know I need to shed this marriage, an eerie reflection of life with my mother. Like a snake sheds its old, worn-out skin once and for all, I will do the same. I decide not to fight for anything except the return of my maiden name. I don't want to bring any of that baggage or memories with me.

Reflecting back, I can see how familiar and easy it was for me to gravitate to him. He was an insecure, passive-aggressive man who struggled in silence with his own depression. All very familiar territory. He used mental and emotional abuse to manipulate and control me. And like Mom, he used distance and isolation as a weapon, withholding himself from me and never sharing what he was struggling with. On my end, I recognized all the familiar torturous and powerless feelings I grew up with.

I'm not surprised that being groomed as a child caregiver led me to this marriage in which I relentlessly tried anything to help him, just like I tirelessly tried to help Mom. Finally, something clicked for me. I suddenly knew in my heart I deserved so much more.

Just like so many other choices I make as a young adult, divorcing Chad is yet another choice that disappoints and upsets my mother. She adores Chad and has adored him from the first time she met him. Regardless of his abuse, which I share with her, he still can do no wrong in her eyes.

"He takes good care of you, Michelle," she reminds me. "There aren't too many men out there who are good like him. And you know, we didn't spend all that money on that beautiful wedding for you to just throw it all away like this."

Once again, she riddles me with massive amounts of guilt and resentment, which only makes my leaving Chad all the more difficult. So difficult that I don't feel welcome at home. As a result, I temporarily move into my grandmother's house until I get my own apartment, since I know that she, unlike my mother, will understand and support me.

CHAPTER 24

Painful Love

A S A YOUNG ADULT IN MY TWENTIES NOW, I can still hear my uncle telling me not to be mad at my mother.

"She doesn't mean to act the way she does," he'd say. "She's ill. She isn't herself when she's ill. You have to try to separate her illness from who she is as a person."

My defensive response would always be served up in a way that would convince you of just how shitty life at home was for me growing up.

"You don't know what life was like with her. You don't understand how hard it was and how mean she was. How can I separate the illness from her when she would hit me for no reason and then I would have to turn around and comfort her when her nerves were totally shot, and she was spiraling out of control? You have no idea what it was like. Life was a roller coaster for me growing up."

Trying to separate my mom from her illness is probably a good idea, but at the time the suggestion fills me with confusion.

What does he know? I think. *He doesn't know what it was like being raised by her and how abusive and mean she could be. He doesn't have a clue.*

I never can separate my mother from her illness. I'm all too consumed with the impact that she has on my emotional and mental state. All I can think about is how even now as a young adult she still manipulates me into doing what she wants. She retains this incredible controlling grip on me, even though I no longer live under her roof. How can that be?

Despite her thumb still being on me from a distance, I still long to find the silver-bullet solution that will get her well. Searching for solutions to help her feel better has just been ingrained since childhood. Like the time I found out about a special kind of doctor who might be able to do something. Someone had told me that a psychopharmacologist could help normalize how Mom was feeling by creating a cocktail of the right drugs. Elated at the news, I ran to tell my father.

This is the missing piece. I found it! I thought as I raced home. *Finally we'll get her the right care.*

"Dad, I found out today that Mom really needs a psychopharmacologist who can diagnose her and give her the right combination of drugs," I exclaim. "This is what she needs. This will make her get well!"

"Michelle, she has a doctor who is already prescribing a variety of drugs to her," Dad replies. "We don't need another doctor."

I try to convince him, but he's not interested. He seems tired and doesn't understand that this will help. Discouraged and upset, I'm forced to let my amazing idea go and continue my mission to search out other ways to help normalize her mood.

Even now as an adult, I can't give up looking for that magic solution to help her, regardless of the mind games she still plays on me.

Our conversations on the phone often leave me thinking about her and the call for hours. She knows how to guilt me into feeling horrible about myself.

"You don't miss me," she says. "If you missed me, you would call and come visit your mother more often."

"Of course I miss you, Mom. You know I love you, but I'm just so busy."

"And when are you going to have grandchildren? I'm going to be dead and gone long before you decide to have any children."

My stomach aches long after our call. Her words leave me angry and depressed at the same time. I'm a mess for days. Maybe that's because I allow her to have such a profound impact on me. Or maybe it's because of her recurring reminder that I've failed to meet my own mother's expectations. Whatever the reason, more often than not I wind up crying hopelessly.

Why does she continue to do this to me and why am I still that same, trapped little girl I once was when I lived at home? It just makes it so hard to love her and, yes, to miss her.

Eventually, the emotional impact of our relationship prompts me to seek out counseling for myself.

After about three months of treatment and my sharing the series of dysfunctional interactions with my mother, my therapist offers me the last piece of advice I would have ever expected.

"You need to limit your interactions with your mother as much as possible," she says. "Your mental well-being is at stake here. You're a different person when you haven't interacted with her as opposed to when you have."

The newfound permission to distance myself from Mom provides me with the validation I've been seeking along with the first glimmer of hope that I might actually create a happier life for myself. Even better, I realize that when I do successfully distance myself from her, it really works. I feel much more peaceful and even a little carefree. The mental exhaustion dissolves.

Of course, that distance is not well received by Mom and the backlash that quickly follows diminishes the benefits of the distance I've worked so hard to put between us. Regardless, I try hard to follow my doctor's advice. This means resisting the urge to answer the phone when she calls me. I have to be on my toes when she calls.

How are you feeling? I ask myself before I pick up.

Only when I'm strong enough to interact with her do I answer. But that's not easy, because I miss her in spite of myself.

Despite the tough history and Mom's abusive nature at times, I find myself wanting to talk to her. Regardless of her volatile moods and her illness, I know she cares deeply about me and wants to know all that is going on in my world. I know how much she loves me as the daughter she fought so hard to have. And when she's in her happy place, my mom is the one person who will allow me to talk about myself endlessly as if it is music to her ears.

When she's that mom, she's the mom I have prayed for. In those instances, I slip into a fantasy world and imagine that one day this will become my permanent and balanced mom. But only now and then do I get to catch a glimpse of her, my old mom. The one I remember from when I was much younger.

There I am sitting perched upon her lap in the kitchen with her arms wrapped around me, hugging me and softly singing to me. I can almost taste the pure sense of love, peace and a normalcy that I clearly took for granted during those earlier years. I'm glad I didn't know about the unpredictable mom who was to follow.

Even now that I'm out of the house, my mother still lashes out at me way more than she ever supports me or shows me love. It's as if she just can't help herself. So although I want to hear her voice, I need to protect myself.

It's so hard to balance that. Having my doctor routinely remind me that I need to guard my mental well-being and the impact my mother has on me helps a great deal. When I'm able to manage the amount of interaction I have with her, I realize what it's like to be peaceful and genuinely in a good mood. Freedom to live life without being manipulated and controlled makes life so much easier. Even joyful. For the first time, I experience a sense of calm and peace. Because this is in such sharp contrast with what I'm used to, it's all the sweeter to experience.

CHAPTER 25

Tasting Happiness and Sorrow

T HAT GIFT OF CONTRAST SHOWS UP for me again not long after.

Acutely reminded by Chad of what I don't want in a relationship, I'm now completely clear about what I'm willing and unwilling to tolerate in a partner.

I'm done with ordinary and done with attracting more of the same from my childhood into my adult life, I decide.

As I sit at the little office desk in my apartment, I begin drafting my very first personal ad to post on Yahoo! Personals. I commit to being truthful and totally honest in my ad. No way am I going to pacify a man by writing something I think he wants to hear. The ad goes something like this:

Single female looking for a smart, responsible and funny man. Seeking someone to enjoy long cups of coffee with on lazy Sunday mornings. Don't even bother responding if you're consumed with football on weekends.

Within a short period of time, my ad speaks to Eddie, a super-sweet man who grew up in the town next to me. Even though he went to all the same places I did as a teen, we never met.

Poison ivy on my face prevents us from getting together for several weeks. My godmother, Aunt Muriel, who helps take me to the doctor, can attest to the fact that I don't even look like myself with my severely swollen eyes and face. There is absolutely no way I will meet him in this condition! Our endless phone calls will have to do.

I start to really like him over the phone. Weeks turn into two months before the poison ivy goes away and we plan our first date. I'm petrified to finally meet him in person. I like him so much that my mind starts to play tricks on me.

He is too good to be true, Michelle, I think one day.

The next day I play a different head game.

Ugh! What do I do if I don't find him attractive?

Thankfully, that's definitely not the case. On Easter eve we finally have our very first date. He's even more handsome in person than in the photo in his personal ad with the cut-off girl's arm wrapped around him.

We date for several months and thoroughly enjoy each other's company as well as the ease of being together. Meeting Eddie raises my happiness bar in ways I could have never imagined. In complete contrast with how hard and emotionally draining life was with both Mom and then Chad, life becomes fun and spontaneous.

Things just get better.

It isn't long before Mom adores my Eddie. She cannot dispute what a remarkable man he is and can see how happy he makes me. Looking back now, I know that her joyful tears on our wedding day reflected her knowing that I was finally happy. I will never forget the smile on her face when she saw the contentment in ours at the ceremony in the little white waterfront church in Waterloo Village.

Unfortunately, this wonderful moment would be overshadowed by what would come later that very same day.

I never thought I would cry anything but tears of jubilation on my wedding day. Blessed by my in-laws with a wedding reception in an elegantly restored picturesque Victorian mansion from the 1800s, we arrive in the cozy building after the ceremony. As we enter the mansion, a crackling fireplace roars on this chilly end-of-November day. The smell of pine boughs lingers in the air from the freshly decorated rooms. Twinkling Christmas trees are positioned in the corners of every room in the mansion. The loft's banister above the main ballroom is beautifully draped with an evergreen garland and red bows, complementing the elegance of the lace-dressed tables below.

As Eddie and I linger with our guests during the cocktail hour, the band begins to play. Gazing out onto the main ballroom floor, I cannot believe that this is our wedding reception. Shortly after we make our grand entrance down the long hallway and stairwell onto the dance floor, I see my mom leaving the reception.

Where is she going? I think.

Moments later I see my father following behind her with her coat and purse. I rush outside into the freezing parking lot in my strapless wedding dress and heels. Eddie follows me.

My parents are sitting in their car as my mother smokes a cigarette.

"Mom, what's wrong?" I ask her.

"I think we're going to go."

"Mom, why? The reception just started," I say. "You can't leave."

"I think I just want to go home."

"Mom, you can't. I haven't even danced my dance with Dad."

She can't even explain to me why she wants to leave. And I know my dad will do whatever she wants him to do regardless of anything I say. I can't win. Even so, I try.

"Dad, you can't leave. I want to have my dance with you," I beg. "Please!"

I turn to Eddie and start crying, envisioning my wedding reception without a dance with my father. They can't leave. Why are they doing this to me? Not today.

Eddie tries to console me. He tells me not to get upset.

"Don't allow her to ruin our special day," he says.

I recognize the words he's speaking, but I can't hear him. All I can hear is my own internal dialogue about how even now, at the age of thirty and on what is supposed to be the happiest day of my life, Mom is still maneuvering so that her desires trump mine.

Somehow, I convince her to stay just long enough for me to have my dance with Dad. That helps, but not enough.

How can she still do this to me? It's just so unfair, I think.

I can't even begin to count how many times that thought has crossed my mind over the past three decades. No matter how old I get or how hard I try to move on, she continues to keep me under her thumb—a reflection that her illness still remains a real struggle for her and for all of us who love her.

CHAPTER 26

An End to the Pain

FOR THE NEXT FEW YEARS, IT CONTINUES to be all about her all the time. She calls continually, even though I have asked her not to during working hours. Doesn't she realize I have a good job now and that I'm trying hard to juggle school at night, too? The expectation to still help Mom feel better and care for her even from a distance weighs heavily on me. At the same time, even my phone calls with her are so toxic that I'm quickly reminded how vital it is for me to protect myself by limiting my interactions with her.

The distance between us definitely does not work for Mom. She continues to call me at the office, where she knows she can reach me. Often. I'm in a no-win situation.

The phone on my desk rings at 10:00 a.m. It's been a busy morning, dealing with a real pain-in-the-butt vendor who clearly doesn't understand that his is not the only project I'm working on at the moment.

Caller identification tells me it's my parents, but I know it's my mom. Dad never calls me. I contemplate not answering because I don't know the kind of mood I'll get from Mom today. Instead, I take a deep breath and pick up.

"Hi, Mom."

There's a long pause.

"Mom?"

Silence again.

Finally, my dad starts talking.

"Michelle, it's Dad. I'm sorry. Your mom passed away this morning."

Without any concern for my colleagues around me, I let out a gut-wrenching scream.

"What do you mean, Dad? How did this happen?"

He begins talking, but all I can hear are my own thoughts.

Oh, my God. My mom is gone forever. I'm never going to be able to hear her voice or see her face.

I pick up the same stack of papers for the third time. Despite all the challenges, despite all the abuse, I loved my mom with all my heart. How can she be gone?

I replay the few moments of connection we shared over the years. I loved that mom. I missed having that mom. And now any dream of having the normal relationship with her I always wanted is over. My mommy is gone forever.

My mind drifts back to her birthday, which we shared together several months earlier.

"Hi, Mom, sorry I'm late. I didn't expect I would be this late. Look what I bought you, Mom. Happy birthday," I say in a rush as I place a large bouquet of the most beautiful yellow roses on the kitchen table and give her a big hug.

"Michelle, they're beautiful," Mom says. "Thank you."

"How are you?" I ask her, my standard check to get a sense of her mood and temperament.

"I'm better now that you're here."

While I appreciate hearing that, the enormous emphasis she puts on my presence burdens me. I quickly move the conversation along.

"Are you ready to go to lunch?"

"Sure," she says.

I take her to lunch at a small Italian bistro and then to get pedicures. Our moments of deep connection are few and far between, but during that lunch we really bond, and I get to fall in love with my mom all over again, the mom I wanted so much and hardly ever got. Now I'll never get her ever again.

Then I reflect on one of our very last conversations. Yet again, I was trying so hard to pull her from the darkness by being cheerful and happy. It wasn't working.

"What is wrong, Mom?"

"Michelle, the days they just come and the days they just go."

"What do you mean, Mom?"

I can't comprehend the resignation in her voice. I can't understand how anyone could give up on life. But it's clear to me that there's nothing I can say this time. Mom has given up the will to live.

So as much as the news of her death surprises me, deep down I knew it was coming. I heard it in her voice.

Just then it hits me that I will no longer be manipulated and tormented by her. There will be no more head games and she can no longer hurt me. That mother is gone now. Forever.

An exhausted sense of release consumes me. I will no longer be under her thumb. I'm finally free.

Loving my sick mother was so very draining. The odd sense of freedom and hope for a better life saddens me as much as it makes me breathe a monster sigh of relief, which is quickly followed by an eerie sense of guilt and confusion. Who feels that way when they lose their own mother?

CHAPTER 27

Not Again

Even with Mom no longer manipulating me because she's gone, the impact of her imprint on me lingers. I realize that I'm not feeling as happy as I once was in my marriage and I have no idea why.

From our fairytale wedding engagement in front of the beautiful Cinderella's castle in Walt Disney World to our Christmas-themed winter wedding in a Victorian mansion, our life had flown off to an amazing start. That was followed by many years of happiness, success and fun, including a magical trip of a lifetime to Bora Bora seven years into our marriage.

As we scrambled off the island boat taxi after a long twenty-three hours of travel, we stepped onto the grounds of the most gorgeous resort. Images of a computer screen saver crossed my mind. This place looked so over-the-top beautiful. I had to pinch myself because it seemed fake.

I wasn't just mesmerized by the seven vivid stripes of cobalt and turquoise waters. I was also intoxicated by the sweet smell of tiare, the local flower adorning the lei wrapped around my neck. Then we entered our water bungalow.

"Look at the floor! Look at the fish in the floor!" I exclaimed as we stared down through the glass floor. Our room was located directly over the lagoon with a spectacularly seductive view of sparkling translucent waters and a rich backdrop of rugged mountains and dense tropical vegetation. Depending on how the sun hit the water, we could see the prettiest emerald green to the deepest blue. One of the volcanic peaks was visible from our oversized king-sized bed that was sprinkled with petals of island flowers.

On our morning bicycle ride to the resort's gorgeous beach-front breakfast, we passed local resort workers on their bikes. They greeted us with warm smiles and a wave. "Ia orana," they would say, which means hello in Tahitian. The friendliness of the island was captured in every experience and interaction we had.

This truly is the most beautiful and happy place on Earth, I thought.

From our private boat trip to a gorgeous remote sand bar to our incredible romantic private moonlit dinner on the beach with the gentle sounds of the calming water lapping onto the shore, every moment from our time in Bora Bora burned into my memory. Talk about romance.

I've come a long way, I thought to myself.

I'm not sure when that sense of romance faded during the next few years. It's not like our marriage was bad. We still shared wonderful times together. Regardless of all the good, however, I realize that I've been compromising the very relationship that once brought me so much joy. Groomed so well to ignore and suppress my own feelings, somewhere along the way I've stopped speaking my truth because I never want to rock the boat.

When I really look at myself, I realize that maybe, just maybe, I've even been placing unspoken expectations on Eddie just as Mom did on me. The problem with unspoken expectations is that nobody can fulfill them.

Of course, I don't say anything. That stupid unwavering commitment to maintaining a sense of calm at any cost overshadows my voice just like it did when I was an eight-year-old girl. And with the silence comes resentment and anger.

Twenty-five-plus years later, after countless hours of therapy and years of self-development work, I'm reverting back to old patterns instilled in me as a child. How can this role still be impacting me in my forties?

I will later figure out that the impact of loving a mentally ill person goes far beyond just caring for them. Who we have to become to care for them can have a gripping effect on our lives for many years to come. The only solution is to continue on with our own healing journey and never get off that path. At the time, however, the lack of communication that results from me avoiding issues in my marriage rather than airing them causes resentment to build up like a pressure cooker. It gets to the point where there is only one place I feel comfortable.

CHAPTER 28

Reality Check

I GRAB A CHOCOLATE DONUT AND STUFF IT in my face as I pass the kitchen. I still love chocolate. It makes me happy and helps me stay in a good mood. I'm going to take the dogs into my pottery shed, the one place where I can escape and get totally lost in the clay. I will make something really magnificent and big today. Maybe I'll throw a large pot or a vase.

Keith Urban plays on my iPhone and I slowly drift into the fantasy world of his love stories. Like a soap opera, I'm consumed by the words of his songs. Before I know it, Sunday afternoon turns into Sunday night, hours from the start of a new workweek where the business of the routine will soon take over.

I'm so glad that I decided to buy my "she shed," where I can be totally me. There's a freedom and a carefree feeling just being in this comfortable little space filled with endless creative possibilities. I have the freedom there to create anything I want. I can throw an oversized vessel or a tiny intricate piece. My time is entirely unscripted.

Working with my hands to create something from nothing is incredibly fulfilling. Equally fulfilling is giving something I've created, nurtured and brought to completion to someone else. I always feel proud handing over something I've made with my own two hands.

Just a few short weeks later, I find myself meeting with a senior leader at work. Mug in hand, I bounce into our corporate offices. After all, it's not every day that you get to meet with a very senior leader at work.

"I brought you a small gift. I'm a potter and made you this mug. I hope you enjoy it," I say as I hand her the bow-adorned mug that's dark brown with a light-pistachio-green glaze.

"Thank you. It's beautiful."

"I have a perfect little she shed in my yard at home where I make all my pottery," I confide. "It's my own little creative sanctuary that's a true reflection of me."

"Girl, I have the whole damn house," she responds. "My entire house reflects me and is filled with all the things that bring me joy."

"That's nice," I reply, thinking how rude she is for being so judgmental of my shed.

What the heck? I just gave her a beautiful mug.

As I leave our meeting, I try hard to dismiss her words, but they stay with me.

CHAPTER 29

The Story of Brayson

A**NOTHER BRUTAL REALITY CHECK FOLLOWS** that one just a week later.

I really don't know how I'm feeling so alive this morning. Today is Day 4 of Date With Destiny. With only four hours of sleep last night, it looks like my Group 13 has been rotated to the front right-hand side of this massive auditorium today. Thousands of people pour into this refrigerator-cold room and quickly fill up the rows of seats allocated to each group, as the leaders stand on chairs waving their oversized posters with group numbers so that people can see where to go.

Today, our team is clear up against the concert-sized speakers just next to the stage. When the music plays through the speakers, my entire body vibrates. Wow, we're so close to the stage today that our leader hands out earplugs. Even better, we're in the direct pathway of where Tony Robbins will walk. Today is relationship day and it's going to be exhilarating. I can already tell!

Tony starts off by sharing with us what we are going to talk about today. Before I know it, he's circling the floor just next to our section. He's so close that I can see how giant he is.

He asks a question and points to a man in the middle section of the floor. A runner quickly hands the man a microphone as Tony asks him his name.

"My name is Brayson."

"Everybody, let's give Brayson a hand!" Tony shouts.

The music plays and we all applaud Brayson, a medium-build man with blond hair who speaks with a very humble tone.

Tony begins talking to Brayson, who shares that he's a military man. He then goes on to admit that he's struggling with life and relationships because he isn't feeling fulfilled.

"Is life about settling?" Tony asks Brayson.

"Absolutely not," Brayson responds.

"What are you made for?" Tony asks.

"I think that people are made to be happy and to contribute," Brayson responds.

Tony asks everyone to sit down and invites all the servicemen and -women to stand up so we can acknowledge them. The music starts to play "I'm proud to be an American, where at least I know I'm free...'Cause there ain't no doubt I love this land, God bless the USA."

The audience roars.

"You had to play that song and make me cry," Brayson says as he wipes the tears from his face.

"It's okay to cry. There is nothing wrong with crying. You're feeling what you deserve to feel along with all the men and women in this room who have served," Tony says.

"Think about this," he continues. "Think about what they had to do to go into battle to do this. How they had to shift their personality to do things that can be scarring on the surface. But there is no scarring on your soul. Yet, there is all this pain and all the failure to get what you want back in this life, where the rules are messy. There, they were painful, but at least you knew how to win. Here, they are so fucking messy. But failure is a bruise, not a tattoo. It's temporary.

"But now you feel impotent because you can't use all your resources because you made a portion of them wrong, when the truth is that it saved other people's lives. What we don't get is reinforcement for that. How often do servicemen and -women and police and firefighters really get acknowledged? It's fucking rare. Oftentimes it's only when there's a fallen comrade."

Brayson gently speaks into his microphone.

"That is why I wear this bracelet."

"What does that represent for you?" Tony asks.

Brayson proceeds to read the bracelet.

"*Staff Sergeant Anthony Davis. Killed in action—Jan 6, 2009.* I have been wearing this bracelet ever since," Brayson shares.

"Why did you pick him?" Tony asks.

"He was a good friend of mine."

"And what would he say to you today if he were here?" Tony asks. "What should you fucking do?"

A big smile comes across Brayson's face. "He'd be like, 'Don't bitch out, man!'"

The audience laughs.

"You know what? You're just fucking tired," Tony says.

"I'm exhausted," Brayson says. "And not only because I've slept ten hours in like four days."

The audience laughs.

"You're just worn out from the conflict of fighting yourself," Tony says. "It's just not fair. You've already battled the real fucking enemy; you don't need a battle within you. The battle is a conflict of ideals. *I need to be this way for this woman. I need to be this way for my son.* Where the fuck am I in this process? And I don't want to be selfish," Tony says.

Tony turns to the audience and asks, "Is this man fucking selfish? Yes or no?"

"No!" the audience yells.

"Yes or no?"

"No!" the audience yells, louder this time.

"Yes or no?"

"No!" the audience yells even louder.

"Well, that's three thousand people from sixty-nine countries who just experienced your essence," Tony says to Brayson.

"Can we all be selfish in the moment, yes or no?" Tony asks the audience.

"Yes," we respond.

"We all can be selfish in moments. But that is not who the fuck we are," Tony declares.

"The mind will make you selfish. But you're not the fucking mind. You can exit the mind, come back to your essence, to your heart and soul, and you can make the tough decisions. The only way we have a life that is magnificent is when we make the tough decisions.

"Anybody can make the easy fucking decisions where it's obvious. The tough decisions where it could be fucking wrong, but you still have to decide what it means to be a leader. That is why you get paid the most if you're in business, that is why you move up, because you can make the fucking painful decisions that no one else has the balls to fucking make. You fucking do it because that is what it means to be a fucking man. And that is what the fuck you are!"

"So listen to your staff sergeant as you carry him on your wrist, because you shared a bond with him," Tony says. "You went into fucking battle and faced death together. He is still here to advise you."

"Fucking Davis," Brayson says.

The audience laughs.

"That's right," Tony says.

"RIP, Cookie," Brayson concludes.

A silence falls over me as Tony hugs him and the music continues to play. I'm unable to hear the thousands of people jumping to their feet and applauding Brayson. It's like everything is muffled and in slow motion.

A profound honesty surfaces within me. I, too, deserve more. I know what it's like to experience that battle of conflicting ideals. I'm living a life to satisfy everyone around me while forgetting about myself. I'm unhappy, an emotion that has surfaced before but one I've learned to quickly suppress and shame myself for feeling. This time I allow it to surface.

Tony tells us that change really happens in the single moment, a moment of decision that causes everything to shift. I have finally hit that threshold he describes, when there's finally enough dissatisfaction to create inner leverage. And in that moment, I hear my brain echo the words I've just heard Tony say: "Not another day. Not another hour. Not another moment!"

Suddenly, I realize that I am done. I'm clear that I am done.

I can hardly breathe. A sinking feeling consumes me. I need to leave the room. Right now. I just want to bolt right out of my chair, but I can't. I'm sitting in the middle of the row with at least ten people sitting on either side. Shit, I'm trapped!

Chocolate, chocolate, chocolate! my mind screams. *I need chocolate.*

But I don't have any chocolate.

I can barely focus. I just want to escape myself right now. Yet part of me really does want that level of happiness that Tony spoke to Brayson about. I hate settling and feeling like I don't have a voice, again. This has become a broken record in my life even now, as an adult. Why?

You, too, should be happy, I think to myself. *You need to stop suppressing your real feelings and speak up for your happiness. You owe it to yourself to speak your truth.*

How can it be that with all the years of therapy, life mistakes and self-development work I have gone through, I'm not finished? What the hell? I thought I had it all figured out and that I was healed. I thought that I had resolved the impact my childhood trauma had on me and my life. Maybe in the back of my mind I always knew that there was still something else to uncover, and more to heal, so that I would no longer compromise my own happiness.

CHAPTER 30

Epiphany

I DON'T KNOW WHAT TO DO, BUT I AM no longer willing to accept the way things are. I need to do something, so I reach out.

Here we go again, I think in the car on the way to my counseling session.

I thought I was done with therapy years ago. I guess I was wrong. All because I just had to keep looking and just had to go to Date With Destiny. Sometimes I wonder why I relentlessly feel the need to probe myself to the point of confusion.

My new therapist's office is situated in a faded old sawmill alongside a dam. The sign for the yoga studio sits at the entrance of the parking lot and reads *Love one another.*

Are you kidding me? Like this isn't hard enough? Easier said than done, I think as I pull into the parking lot.

I park along the edge of the pebble-covered parking lot in clear view of a beautiful waterfall just behind the building. The rushing waters off the cliff aggressively pound down onto the rocks in pursuit of a journey forward toward the calmer opening of the stream.

The modest timbered building stands alone around a small curved road. I enter and take the tall, narrow staircase to the second floor. At the top of the landing, I pass a modest seating area and turn down a small hallway, at the end of which I find the therapist's office. He greets me at the door and invites me in.

The room is small and quite warm due to the afternoon sun spilling in from the oversized windows overlooking the dam. The vaulted ceiling helps make the space feel airy and welcoming.

We exchange awkward pleasantries as I take a seat on the worn and sunken couch. The counselor looks at me with an encouraging smile. He seems nice enough. I notice a small armchair adjacent to the couch that we are on, which is filled with little stuffed animals. That seems odd.

He must also counsel children, I think.

But I don't consider it any further because I'm consumed with anticipation about how this first session will go.

He looks at me and smiles, his legs crossed and a notepad and a pen on his lap.

"Today I'm just going to get to know you through a series of questions," he says. "It's helpful to gain an understanding of your childhood and life experiences. So tell me. What was your childhood like?"

"It was interesting," I respond. "It was hard growing up with a bipolar mother, but I survived and have come to realize I'm actually much stronger for that experience. I have done a lot of reflecting and self-development work over the past several years and I can see the impact it has had on my life. But it does not define where I'm going."

I proceed to talk to him about my dissatisfaction with my marriage. Then, something weird happens.

The therapist takes one of the stuffed animals off the chair next to me. He happens to grab the small stuffed lion and holds it in his lap.

What is he doing? I think. *Why is he holding a stuffed animal?*

Handing me the stuffed animal, he says, "This is my heart

and I'm going to give it entirely to you to take care of, completely. I'm going to trust you to take care of my heart. Okay? I'm
going to give you all of the responsibility."

This is strange, I think. *I'm sitting here holding a stuffed animal that represents someone's heart.*

That is when it hits me.

*Oh, my goodness! Maybe that has been what's been going on
with me! Eddie cannot possibly be responsible for taking care of my
every need.*

"When one person relies on the other person to meet nearly
all their emotional needs, a codependent environment is created," the counselor explains. "You give the one you love the ac-
countability and responsibility of taking care of your needs 100
percent."

I know this place. It's very familiar for me. It's my home. I'm
a child of codependency.

Suddenly I'm ten years old again sitting at the dinner table
with my mom and dad.

"Well, you have two weeks to get ready," Dad says to Mom
and me. "We're leaving for St. Thomas on the 21st."

Mom hadn't been very happy lately. I tried to make her
laugh and talk to her without any success. But Dad knew that
getting her away to a beautiful island would put her in a good
mood, even if only temporarily. He knows her and loves to bring
her happiness and fulfillment regardless of the consequences,
even if he has no idea how to pay for the trip.

Mom never owned her own contentment. In her pursuit to
find things that pacified her and made the time pass, she placed
her stuffed lion in Dad's lap and in mine.

Isn't it natural that this is what I do now as an adult? My observations of my parents along with my own experiences perfectly groomed me to act this way. This is my normal. I bring others fulfillment just doing what I know.

Now I can see that there's another way to do things, one that I've never been taught.

I could beat myself up about that. Instead, I find myself being mildly proud as I reflect on the many years of self-discovery I've invested in myself. The efforts I've made to discover what makes me happy and brings me fulfillment that have brought me to this point. I've learned how important it is for me to make time for my pottery, my volunteer work, my exercising.

I'm further along than I thought, I think.

Yet it seems that I have so much more work to do.

CHAPTER 31

Renewal

I'M NOT THE ONLY ONE WANTING TO work on myself, as it turns out.

"I've decided I'm going to do the Landmark Forum," Eddie says as we walk the dogs at our favorite park. "Tomorrow, I'm going to register."

I'm shocked but so grateful that he has made this decision for himself. I've always wanted him to take this life-changing program. For years I had begged him to go. Instead, I found myself having to defend the program to him countless times.

I'm overjoyed for him now because I know what is possible.

Day 1 of the Forum ends. At about midnight he makes it home and creeps upstairs into the bedroom. As he walks into the dimly lit bedroom, I can see that he looks different. His eyes are sparkling, and he's smiling from ear to ear. I immediately sense that something major and profound has shifted for him.

He even talks to me differently.

"It was amazing!" he says. "All of it. Just amazing. That David Cunningham is phenomenal!"

"Wow, really?" I respond. Then I just shut up and listen. I don't want to interrupt what he is about to share.

"It was so powerful. I'm totally and completely exhausted, but I can see why you like this work. It's really cool."

I can't believe my ears or my eyes.

He just looks so light and at ease. So peaceful. All I can pick up is a massive sense of calm. We lie in bed and over the next few hours he shares with me the conversations from the day. He's totally invigorated by the many messages he heard.

My heart is full. I'm so happy for him because this is only the end of Day 1 and there are two and a half more days to go. I can only imagine what else he will gain from his experience.

Eddie invites me to the Sunday evening session. As a Landmark graduate, I have gone to many of these evening sessions, but in all my years of volunteering for Landmark, I have never been so excited to attend one. Eddie comes bounding up to me as I enter the room. He looks amazing. He doesn't seem at all tired. Even more impressive, he doesn't appear at all burdened. That stress that he's carried for so long has totally disappeared.

He smiles the biggest warm smile at me and then hugs me.

"I feel amazing," he says. "This has been such a great program."

I'm looking at a transformed man, a man filled with new possibilities for the future who is at complete ease with everything. I never imagined he would gain so much.

An awakening happens when you do the Landmark Forum. Something shifts and causes you to come away with a new perspective about life. In the program, you rid yourself of the limiting beliefs and stories you've told yourself. You gain a new freedom and sense of power to be effective in the areas of your life that matter most to you. And you come away with a conviction and new level of confidence with which you live your life. As a result, a renewed zest for life emerges. I remember feeling it all and wanting the same for all my loved ones immediately because it was so delicious and empowering. Little do I know the impact that this experience and my continued healing will have on our happiness together.

CHAPTER 32

Reconnecting

IT'S HARD FOR EDDIE'S LEVITY AND zest for life not to spill over on me. Following the Landmark Forum, we both realize that we need to get away and reconnect. We decide to return to St. John in the U.S. Virgin Islands, where we honeymooned fourteen years before.

We feel like we're going home to the place where it all started. Our beachfront accommodations and three nights and four days of the powdery white-sand beaches and crystal-clear blue waters of the Caribbean await us. I'm so excited! Ever since I was a young girl, there has been something magical about the blue Caribbean waters that I've savored. As a teen I can remember taking close-up photos of the beaches and the blue water so that I could remember how amazing it was to be there. I can't wait to reconnect with Eddie in this place that is so special to us.

As we walk into our oceanfront room, I can't believe my eyes. The water is literally just outside of the bedroom door, and the calm, pristine turquoise-blue waters are just lapping up on the perfectly white beach. I can already tell that these next few days are going to be amazing. Spending uninterrupted time together hasn't always been easy. While it was nice to be on vacations in the past, small irritations would somehow always surface. This trip feels different. Just eating breakfast and swimming in the ocean feels different. We're not only genuinely enjoying each other's company, we're connecting on a deeper level. The undercurrent of upset and irritation that once lived there is now gone. Instead, there's a sense of ease being together now that feels so wonderful.

Before we know it, our time on the island comes to a close. We declare that we'll return in the fall to celebrate our fifteenth wedding anniversary together, and when we do, it will be for a longer visit. When we get home, life continues on the same positive path. Interactions are loving and tender, and our communication continues to improve. What a shift! I'm beyond grateful.

CHAPTER 33

Fire Walkers

Life continues to unfold as if magically. Eddie and I both decide to do Tony Robbins' Unleash the Power Within. I was already attending as a staff volunteer, so Eddie deciding that he wants to attend with me couldn't be more perfect.

As a Tony Robbins Crew member, I get to support the big fire walk that happens on the first day of the event. The fire walk is a powerful portion of the program where participants are primed and empowered to walk across hot coals. During my first day of training, I learn my role on the fire lane. We spend hours in the training and even more hours rehearsing the actual walk and how to support the attendees. I had no idea this level of training went into the fire walk. With every hour that I train, I gain more and more confidence about how to support the walkers.

Since there are fourteen thousand participants, there will be thirty-three fire lanes set up to ensure that everyone can walk across the coals. I'm taking my role very seriously because I want everyone, including my Eddie, to have an incredible experience. Walking on the hot coals two years ago turned out to be such an empowering experience. I want that for everyone who comes down our Lane 32.

Levi, my lane partner, and I have the job of organizing the line and keeping the participants in the focused frame of mind, also known as *state*, and ready for their walk. He knows that Eddie is here and how excited I am for my husband to walk the coals. I ask him to keep an eye out for him, but I have very little hope he will find him among all the people. And even though I tell Eddie that I'm in Lane 32, the lanes are not marked and it's quite dark in the parking lot where the fire lanes are located.

At 1:00 a.m. the drummers start to drum, and their drumming becomes very loud. Tony starts to speak on the microphone and helps keep the energy in the crowd going. Then the drumming kicks in with more intensity. All of a sudden, I look up and a giant sea of attendees is rushing through the gates toward the fire lanes. I have honestly never seen so many people in one space before. I try my best to direct people and smile and chant *Yes!* to keep them in state. All of a sudden, Levi comes down the side of our lane.

Oh, great, I think. *I'm doing something wrong. Maybe I'm not where I'm supposed to be.*

Nope. Instead of chastising me, he pulls me up to the front of the line and there is Eddie, just getting ready to walk. I cannot believe that he found him! I get to watch Eddie walk across the coals! Oh, my gosh, this is amazing.

As Eddie stands at the entrance to the coals, he focuses his eyes upward. The fire lane chief shouts in his ear and tells him to go. Tears start to roll down my cheeks. I'm getting to watch him walk across fire. What a gift this is for me.

He effortlessly walks across the coals and the team on the end of the lane catches him perfectly, just like we rehearsed. It's amazing! With a big smile on his face, he turns to me and waves goodbye. I have the rest of my lane to get back to now and he is headed home.

We have both walked across fire, I think. *I will never forget that.*

I just love that Tony uses the fire walk as a metaphor to help us realize that we can overcome any kind of fear that lives in the head. Su, my Tony Robbins coach, always reminds me to stay out of my head and to listen to my heart.

"Get in your head and you're dead," Tony says, because when you go into your head you believe the most limiting thoughts. The brain is just not wired to make you happy—it's wired for survival. Each time we think a thought, it correlates to an emotion. So we can think a thought and feel stressed, or we can think a thought and feel loved. This is why Tony stresses that we must train our brains. In his three-and-a-half-day Unleash the Power Within program, he embeds in us the importance of having our mind serve us so that it won't be able to run us. We don't want to negotiate with our mind, he insists. We just need to declare what we want and do it. But that means coming to terms with ourselves on every level.

CHAPTER 34

Courage Over Fear

I CONTINUE WITH MY DEEP DIVE INTO myself. Soon I realize that my marriage isn't the only part of my life I'm settling for. Somewhere along the way, I've also compromised my creative energy for a good-enough job that's slowly extinguishing my creative light. Similar to my marriage, I toggle between *How dare you complain or want more?* and *You should be happy with what you have, because you have more than most.*

But my marriage has set the precedent for what I will no longer tolerate, and my speaking up in that situation somehow gives me the confidence to speak up for what I want professionally.

Just then, I'm presented with the opportunity to have a project planning meeting with an admirable woman and senior director. Over the years, I've witnessed her assorted initiatives and how excitingly inventive those projects are for her and the company. I get excited just thinking about that exact kind of endeavor.

"I want to work for you," I say to her over lunch as we review an upcoming meeting agenda we're collaborating on. "I'm so creative, and you're working on such wonderfully innovative projects. One day, if you'll have me, maybe I can be part of your operation. I just wanted to tell you how much I would love that. I hope that's okay."

I can't believe I've put voice to those words. I just showed her all my cards. Oh, my gosh, what if she thinks I'm nuts? Or too forward? What if she totally rejects me?

She doesn't say much. She just smiles, and we quickly move along to the next topic we need to cover during our lunch meeting. We have a lot to get done.

Her reaction leaves me feeling less than optimistic. Consumed by work, I forget about that lunch.

One morning a couple of months after my bold approach, I wake up feeling energized. I'm not sure why. I get dressed in my usual manner and head out to walk my dogs at the local park. As we wander through the woods to the opening of the small pond, a cool breeze sweeps across my face. There is a crispness about the air after the intense storm last night. The dogs run down the path in pursuit of two squirrels chasing each other up a tree.

As I look out across the pond, which is beautiful this morning, I don't even realize I'm thinking about my job. Suddenly, a distinct clarity comes over me.

That's it. I need a new challenge, I think. *I'm done. I am totally done.*

Then I say it out loud to the pond.

"I am done!"

With those words, what feels like a boulder lifts. I've finally connected with my truth and just told it to the pond, and I feel positively buoyant. I guess I've finally hit my tipping point. I don't know what this means, but I'm finished settling for what life hands me. It's time to take the actions I need to be truly happy in all facets of my existence.

I realize that I'm ready to walk away. I'm ready to leave and give up all that I have achieved at work because I now know it's not what I want.

Hours later, I'm back at my desk working away on a really challenging project. I'm far from energized by the mundaneness of the job. The work never seems to end, with emails and requests coming in to me faster than I can address them.

One step at a time, Michelle, I say to try to calm myself. I force myself to stop for a second and reflect on the morning's beautiful pond.

All of a sudden, an instant message from my boss pops up.

Oh, no, I think. *I hope there isn't another fire that needs attention.*

She asks me if I can talk to her over the phone, so I call her. Sounding weird and yet happy, she proceeds to tell me about an opportunity that she feels could be a great fit for me. The role includes working on a very creative development project. My jaw hits my desk.

"What?" I ask in total disbelief. "What do you mean?"

She continues on, then asks if I would be open to exploring the opportunity. She's willing to support me if I am. Oh, my gosh, this is a dream come true. I compose myself enough to respond.

"Yes, I'm very open to exploring this opportunity," I say, echoing her words because I'm so overwhelmed that I can't think of any fresh ones.

I hang up the phone in complete disbelief. Just a few months ago, I openly expressed my desire to work in a more creative space for the first time. I had no idea how or if this would ever happen. Then, I find myself at the park this morning having a major epiphany about my happiness at work. And now this phone call?

This must be the result of my speaking from my heart, I think. *Again.*

CHAPTER 35

Truth

W<small>E DON'T GET TO CHOOSE THE FAMILIES</small> we're born into. Our childhood reality is one that we are forced to accept. But the programming that takes place in our young minds does not have to dictate our entire lifetimes. My thirst for knowledge and deep desire for self-discovery had me persevere forward to really learn about myself. The person who once lived in the shadows of others' needs will no longer dwell in that space.

"Bless the thing that broke you down and cracked you open because the world needs you open," wrote Rebecca Campbell.

Obstacles tested me every step of the way. They tested how badly I wanted freedom from my past and the limiting thoughts they were accompanied by. An assortment of excuses could have easily interrupted my journey and prevented me from reaching the other side. It has been a long process of stepping forward, stumbling backward and then standing back up to press forward yet again. But that perseverance finally allowed me to break through the relentless walls and thought patterns that had me stay small.

I no longer accept the status quo. I have broken the miserable cycle of being passive and unhappy that did not bring me the fulfillment and joy I deserved. I have discovered my own personal power, connected with my truth and found the voice to speak up. I no longer settle, and I believe in my heart that I can actively define what I want for myself. I commit to consciously reach for it. Connecting to my truth has made me unstoppable. Instead of fearing risk, I will dance with it. I won't allow excuses to stop me from going for what I want. I get to re-create my reality as often as I wish.

That reality includes creating a vehicle to heal by giving back. Recognizing that I wanted to give children the sense of self-esteem I missed during my own childhood, I came up with the idea for a project to empower kids. I named it Perfect, Just the Way You Are.

In partnership with wonderful leadership at Johnson & Johnson (J&J), we turned that idea into reality and designed a powerful after-school enrichment program for employees to deliver in their communities. In the program, which is designed to combat bullying from the space of strength and self-love, the children gain a sense of confidence and leave the program with bolstered self-esteem.

Perfect has been a true labor of love for me since its inception in 2013. Our after-school enrichment program offers children the opportunity to connect to their passion and celebrate their individuality, while learning leadership skills and understanding the importance of a nourished body and nourished mind.

Every time we run that program, I have the chance to confront the thoughts that still surface from my youth and to heal. By helping kids to realize their own greatness, I help myself to realize mine. I know those limiting thoughts and fears will still creep in. But I have learned that they become softer when I focus on helping others, and by listening to my heart I allow myself to be guided by that truth.

I've come to realize that I'm done settling. This is an enormous shift for me. Making myself a priority is in sharp contrast with my childhood, when everybody came before me. At the age of forty-six, I'm finally realizing that this life I have been given is up to me. That means making my happiness the priority, without guilt. I'm not here to service someone else or make everything okay for others before me. I am clear that I want to create the most amazing life possible for myself and I am not willing to accept anything less.

As a child caregiver to a mother with a mental illness, I'm also realizing that the long-term impact of loving her lingers on to this day. I must stay in inquiry of myself and always pursue ongoing self-discovery. As a caregiver, I was groomed to deal with life differently than most. There is no autopilot for me. Instead I must relentlessly seek to grow, expand, push those boundaries and explore those unhealthy beliefs I know will reappear in my life. By doing this, I know I will strengthen my muscle so that I can catch myself quicker when I slide backward. That will only empower me to create the life I deserve.

This is a very different message from the one I thought I would be imparting when I set out on this journey. I thought this book would merely share how to cope with a life compromised as a result of loving someone with a mental illness. Instead, I have learned that although I am a work in progress, I have persevered, and triumphantly emerged from a dark and challenging past. I hope this message reminds us all that we *can* thrive in the face of past adversity. We just have to have the courage to look inside and challenge the ingrained conditioning that doesn't serve us.

EPILOGUE

I CANNOT DISPUTE THE NEGATIVE IMPACT Mom's illness has had on me throughout my life. Those experiences have shaped who I am as a person. However, after years of self-discovery, therapy and reflection, I now realize how growing up with my bipolar mother also positively serves me every day. That's not something I have always been able to see, let alone appreciate.

Without those experiences and challenges, I might not be as focused and determined to better understand myself and to become the best version of myself. This includes constantly seeking to elevate my level of contribution in whatever I set out to accomplish. I also appreciate the depths of compassion that I have for others, along with my super-strong willingness to really hear and understand people.

My trials with Mom altered my own disposition about life. My zest for life was born out of seeing Mom's pain and her inability to embrace the basic beauty of each new day. Intuitively, I now seek out the good in others and see the glass of life as half full. I know how to create my own sunshine on a cloudy day.

Finally, I really appreciate my insatiable hunger to make a difference in the world. I do what I can to help stop suffering among children as well as among those struggling with mental illness or caring for those with mental illness. In that vein, I hope

I can help you avoid some of the pain I've endured by sharing my story along with the recommendations that follow.

My Message to Caregivers

I'm not a medical or trained professional, and you will always want to seek professional support and guidance for your unique situation. But the advice below, based on my experience with my mother, was gained the hard way. May these suggestions ease your path:

- Support people challenged by mental illness to get the treatment they need and deserve.
- Recognize that loved ones suffering from mental illness are not defined by their condition. See the person, not the illness.
- Know that their illness is not about you. The way they may treat you is not a reflection of you, so don't take it personally.
- Love them, but remember to protect your own well-being so that you can be there for them. Make time to nourish yourself and learn to set the boundaries you need for your own well-being.

Be Sure You Take Care of Yourself

See my website for best practices for yourself. (breakingintomylife.com/2017/12/04/best-practices-for-yourself/)

Together, We Can Make a Difference

We can all play a bigger part in fostering a new, empowering conversation that will make a real difference in how people relate to mental illness. The current stigma means that people suffer silently without seeking the help they need. I know that together, we can all help to eliminate that stigma. We can cultivate an open conversation about mental illness at home, at work and in our schools. Here are some ways to help make a difference.

At home:
- Foster compassion and a safe space of open dialogue. Open communication is contagious. If you do it, you will encourage others to do the same.
- Adopt self-care and well-being practices in the home that include good nutrition, exercise, mindfulness, connection with others and enjoyable hobbies.
- Check in with loved ones and see how they are feeling.
- As I mentioned above, recognize that loved ones suffering from mental illness are not their condition. See the person, not the illness.

At work:
- Promote awareness of mental health and foster compassion and a safe space of open dialogue. It bears repeating: Open communication is contagious. If you do it, you will encourage others to do the same.
- Spearhead education initiatives to help raise awareness about mental health. Include topics like being conscious of language, how to foster equality in people's perception of mental illness as compared with physical illness and the importance of compassion for those suffering with mental illness.
- Establish a mental health resource group for which employees can volunteer in order to foster a body of staff that can help to organically cultivate a culture of awareness and compassion.

- Provide mental health first aid training to help employees identify signs and empower peers to support each other.
- Have an employee assistance program that employees can easily access.
- Ensure adequate mental health benefits coverage for employees.
- Once again, recognize that sufferers are not their condition. See the person, not the illness.

At school:
- Cultivate an environment of empathy and compassion toward each other.
- Promote an environment of positive self-esteem and self-love.
- Empower and celebrate diversity, talent and the skills of all students, so they realize their own unique greatness.
- Start a mental health awareness conversation in your school.
- Coordinate initiatives, including a Mental Health Awareness Day/Week, to help raise awareness.
- Declare your school to be a stigma-free institution.
- Understand the warning signals for suicide.

Be Aware of the Signs of Depression and Suicide
Whether at home, at work or at school, we all need to be able to recognize the signs and symptoms of depression, which include:
- Prolonged sadness
- Hopelessness
- Irritability
- Being consumed by feelings of worthlessness or guilt
- Low energy and fatigue—moving slowly

- Little or no interest in hobbies or activities
- Restlessness
- Inability to focus or concentrate
- Difficulty making decisions or recalling things
- Unusual sleep patterns
- Unusual weight changes or shift in appetite
- Suicidal thoughts or attempts

We also need to be able to recognize the signs of suicide, as suicide is the tenth-leading cause of death in the U.S., according to the American Foundation for Suicide Prevention. These include:

- Comments made about harming themselves or saying things like *I don't want to be here*
- Seeming withdrawn from loved ones
- Unpredictable moodiness or aggressive behavior
- Increased drug or alcohol use
- Engaging in conversations or having thoughts about death
- Unpredictable and unsafe behavior
- If you or someone you know is at immediate risk for suicide, call the National Suicide Prevention Lifeline at 800-273-TALK (8255) or call 911 immediately.

Talk About Mental Illness Openly

Increased knowledge and ongoing, open conversations are the two weapons that we have when it comes to destigmatizing mental illness. We all have the power to create a different kind of conversation, but that won't happen without us. Conversations can lead to making a real difference in someone's life. And that can lead to positive change in ridding mental illness of the stereotypes and prejudice, paving the way for a space where people no longer suffer in silence. Everyone deserves the opportunity to have the best possible quality of life. Together, we can help make that happen.

Made in the USA
Middletown, DE
25 February 2018